Information Management Strategy of the Prophet {PBUH}

Prof Javed Iqbal Saani

PhD, MBA (MIS), MBA (Finance), BBA (Bus Admin)

Intellectual Capital Enterprise Limited, London

Copyright © 2019 Prof Javed Iqbal Saani
All rights reserved.
No reproduction of the book in any form such as electronic, photocopying, scanning, recording or otherwise. It also includes storing for retrieval purpose or transmitting through electronic media i.e., email. Prior written permission of the publisher may require doing any of the above under the relevant act that follows the Copyright, Design, and Patent Act 1988.
Authors and the publisher are not responsible for any damage caused by the application/use of the concepts, techniques, instruction, or actions. The authors and publisher refuse any implied warranties or related matters.

ISBN: 9781710682380

Published by Intellectual Capital Enterprise Limited, ICE Kemp House, 152-160 City Road, London, EC1 V2N
Printed in England with the collaboration of Amazon.co.uk.

CONTENTS

About the author	vii
Dedication	xvii
Acknowledgment	xix
Preface	xxi

1 INTRODUCTION TO INFORMATION MANAGEMENT — 25

Introduction	25
A-Methods of capturing information	25
1- Scouting before the battle of Badr	25
2-Catching the enemy spy	26
3- Sending a companion	27
4- Deputing a soldier	28
5-Through the intelligence personnel	28
B-Methods of dissiminating information	29
1- Umar (RA) for lifting the siege of Ta'if	29
2-Two envoys for the news of victory of Badr	29
3-Deputation of key personnel to answer Abu Syufyan	30
4-Ali (RA) as special representative	30
5-Through letters	31
C- Sources of information	31
Devine revelation	32

Deployment of personnel ... 34
Seeking secrecy of information — 34
Methods of saving information — 35
2 CASE STUDY: THE CONQUEST OF MAKKAH — 37
The brief account of the expedition — 37
Preparation ... 37
Muslim at the outstrips of the destination ... 39
Islamic army took the control of Makkah ... 42
The information strategy — 43
Collecting information ... 43
Processing information ... 44
Storage mechanism ... 45
Dissemination ... 45
Secrecy of information — 46
Alternative view — 46
Deputation of a small squadron — 48
The Devine help — 48
3 CASE STUDY: THE BATTLE OF HUNAIN — 51
The brief account of the battle — 51
Muslims advance ... 52
Muslims won the day ... 53
Concerns of Ansar ... 55
The information strategy — 56
Capturing Information ... 57
Spies of the enemy ... 58

Observation 58
Dissemination of information 58
Record keeping 59

4 CASE STUDY: THE TABUK COMPAIGN 63
The brief account the compaign 63
Background 64
Preparations 65
The expedition and its impacts 67
The information Startegy 67
Information management 68
Gathering information 68
Written communication 69
Dissemination of information 71

5 CASE STUDY: THE TREATY OF HODHABIA 73
The brief account of the event 73
The drivers of the campaign 73
The negotiation 75
The glad tidings of victory 76
The inforamtion strategy 77
Managing information 77

6 CASE STUDY: THE HIJRAH EXPEDITION 81
The story the expedition 81
Background 81
Preparation 84
The journey 86
Towards Madinah 89

v

Information management (IM)   **92**

    Collection   92

    Secrecy of information   93

    Dissemination   94

Bibliography   *97*

Index   *103*

Other Books by the Author (S)   *109*

  Islamic Management Style   109

  Management Sciences   112

  General interest   113

NOTES   *149*

About the author

Javed Iqbal was a resident of Rawalakot (AJ&K). He received his Ph.D. from the University of Salford and an MBA (Information Management) from the University of Hull. Previously Dr. Iqbal received a BBA and an MBA (in Finance) from the University of AJ&K, both with distinction. The University of Azad Jammu & Kashmir, Muzaffarabad (AJ&K) awarded him two gold medals for his educational performance. The government of Pakistan selected him for higher education and deputed him to the UK to complete his doctorate. The government of Pakistan awarded him $100, 000 for it.

Professor Iqbal joined IQRA University Islamabad campus as an associate professor in 2006. He became the head of Department of Technology Management in International Islamic University Islamabad (IIUI) in 2012. Dr. Iqbal joined AKU (AJ&K) as a professor in 2015 and has been appointed as a Dean Faculty of Management Sciences.

His article titled "Learning from a Doctoral Research Project: Structure and Content of a Research Proposal" has been ranked by the Deakin University of Australia as the best piece of research for doctoral students. The research paper is immensely popular. Dr. Javed Iqbal has been nominated by an international organization for the Award of Distinguished Scientist for his research contribution. Professor Iqbal has published twenty-two research articles and forty-three books so far. He has developed an interest in Islamic Leadership Style recently. Professor Iqbal has published in such International Journals as *Electronic Journal of Business Research Methods*, *European Journal of Social Sciences*, *Œconomica*, and *European Journal of*

Scientific Research. His books on various subjects are available on Amazon, details are at the end of the book.
You can reach him @ iqbalsaani@gmail.com
Website: javediqbalsaani.wordpress.com

Value of knowledge I

Say (to them, O Muhammad(ﷺ)): Are those who know equal with those who know not? But only men of understanding will pay heed. [Az-Zumar: 9]

Value of knowledge II

Anas (May Allah (SWT) be pleased with him) reported: The Messenger of Allah (SWT) (ﷺ) said, "He who goes forth in search of knowledge is considered as struggling in the Cause of Allah (SWT) until he returns." [At- Tirmidhi].

Value of knowledge III

Abu Hurairah (May Allah (SWT) be pleased with him) reported: Messenger of Allah (SWT) (ﷺ) said, "Verily! The world is accursed and what it contains is accursed, except remembrance of Allah (SWT) and those who associate themselves with Allah (SWT); and a learned man, and a learning person." [At- Tirmidhi, Book 1, Hadith 478

Value of Knowledge IV

Abu'd-Darda' (رضي الله عنه) said, "I heard the Messenger of Allah (SWT), (ﷺ), say,

1. 'Allah (SWT) will make the path to the Garden easy for anyone who travels a path in search of knowledge.
2. Angels spread their wings for the seeker of knowledge out of pleasure for what he is doing.
3. Everyone in the heavens and everyone in the earth asks forgiveness for a man of knowledge, even the fish in the water.

4. The superiority of the man of knowledge to the man of worship is like the superiority of the moon to all the planets.

5. The men of knowledge are the heirs of the Prophet (ﷺ)'s.

6. The Prophet (ﷺ)'s bequeath neither dinar nor dirham; they bequeath knowledge. Whoever takes it has taken an ample portion.'"

[Abu Dawud and at-Tirmidhi; Riyadh us Salihin, Hadith 1388, p. 211]

Qualities of good leader/manager I
It was by the mercy of God that you were lenient with them (O Muhammad (ﷺ)), for if you had been severe and hard-hearted, they would have forsaken you. So, pardon them and ask (God's) forgiveness for them and consult with them upon the conduct of affairs. [Al-e-Imran: 159]

Qualities of good leader/manager II
Hadhrat Ibn 'Umar (رضي الله عنه) reports that Rasulullah (ﷺ) said "Three persons are such as will have no fear of the horrors of the Day of Judgement, nor they will be required to render an account. They will stroll merrily on mounds of musk until the people are relieved of rendering their account. One is a person who learned the Qur'an, merely seeking Allah (SWT)'s pleasure and therewith leads people in salat in a manner that they are pleased with him; the second person is the one who invites men to salaat for the pleasure of Allah (SWT) alone. <u>The third person is the one who has fair dealings between him and his master, as well as between himself and his subordinates</u>" [Quoted by Al-Tibrani in Al-Majam Al-Slaasa; Fazail-e-Amaal, Virtues of the Holy Qur'an, Hadith 36]

Qualities of good leader/manager III
Abdullah ibn-e-'Umar Radiyallahu 'anhuma narrates that a person came to Nabi (ﷺ) and asked: O Rasulullah (ﷺ)! How many times may I forgive my servant? Nabi remained silent. <u>The man asked again: O Rasulullah (ﷺ)! How many times may I</u>

forgive my servant? He replied: Everyday seventy times. (Tirmidhi) Note: In Arabic, the figure 'seventy' is used to express too many in number. [Muntakhib Ahadith, p. 415]

Striving for the cause of Allah (SWT)

Narrated Abu Hurairah: A man from the Companions of the Prophet (ﷺ) passed by ravine containing a small spring of thirst-quenching water, so he was amazed by how pleasant it was. So, he said: 'I should leave the people and stay in this ravine. But I will not do it until I seek permission from the Messenger of Allah (ﷺ).' So, he mentioned that to the Messenger of Allah (ﷺ), and he said: 'Do not do so. **For indeed one of you standing in the cause of Allah (SWT) is more virtuous that his Salat in his house for seventy years.** Do you not love that Allah (SWT) forgive your sins and admit you into Paradise? Then fight in the cause of Allah (SWT), for whoever fights in Allah's (SWT) cause for the time it takes for two milking of a camel, then Paradise is obligatory for him.'" [Jami` at-Tirmidhi: English translation: Vol. 3, Book 20, Hadith 1650]

Greatness of Allah (SWT), the Exalted

In the name of Allah (SWT), the Beneficent, the Merciful.
1. All that is in the heavens and the earth glorifieth Allah (SWT); and He is the Mighty, the Wise. 2. His is the Sovereignty of the heavens and the earth; He quickeneth and He giveth death, and He can do all things. 3. He is the First and the Last, and the Outward and the Inward, and He is Knower of all things. 4. He is Who created the heavens and the earth in six Days; then He mounted the Throne. He knoweth all that entereth the earth and all that emergeth therefrom and all that cometh down from the sky and all that ascendeth there, and He is with you wheresoever ye may be. And Allah (SWT) is Seer of what ye do. 5. His is the Sovereignty of the heavens and the earth, and unto Allah (SWT) (all) things are brought back. 6. He causeth the night to pass into the day, and He causeth the day to pass into the night, and He is the knower of all that is in the breasts. [Al-Hadidh: 1-6]

Allah (SWT) likes those who loves one another.
Yahya related to me from Malik from Abu Hazim ibn Dinar that Abu Idris al-Khawlani said, "I entered the Damascus mosque and there was a young man with a beautiful mouth and white teeth sitting with some people. When they disagreed about something, they referred it to him and proceeded from his statement. I inquired about him, and it was said, 'This is Muadh ibn Jabal.' The next day I went to the noon-prayer, and I found that he had preceded me to the noon prayer, and I found him praying."

Abu Idris Al-Khaulani (May Allah (SWT) had mercy upon him) reported: I once entered the mosque in Damascus. I happened to catch sight of a young man who had bright teeth (i.e., he was always seen smiling). Several people had gathered around him. When they differed over anything, they would refer it to him and act upon his advice. I asked who he was, and I was told that he was Mu'adh bin Jabal (May Allah (SWT) be pleased with him) The next day I hastened to the mosque but found that he had arrived before me and was busy in performing Salat. I waited until he finished, and then went to him from the front, greeted him with Salam and said to him, "By Allah (SWT) I love you." He asked, "For the sake of Allah (SWT)?" I replied, "Yes, for the sake of Allah (SWT)". He again asked me, "Is it for Allah's (SWT) sake?" I replied, "Yes, it is for Allah's (SWT) sake." Then he took hold of my cloak, drew me to himself and said, "Rejoice! I heard Messenger of Allah (ﷺ) saying, **'Allah, the Exalted, says: My love is due to those who love one another for My sake, meet one another for My sake, visit one another for My sake and spend in charity for My sake"**. [Riyad as-Salihin: English book reference: Book 1, Hadith 382] (Muwatta Malik: English reference: Book 51, Hadith 15)

Dedication

To my parents who invested heavily for our education and remained engaged in prayers for our success and wellbeing.

Acknowledgment

Special gratitude is due to all those who helped me to compile the work. I am grateful to my family who spared me to embark on the project. They also supply valuable information which enriched the contents of this effort. May Allah (SWT) reward them for their contribution? Ameen!

Preface

All prayers to Allah (SWT), the exalted, slat wa slam to all the Prophet (AS) especially upon the last (ﷺ), mercy and blessings upon his noble companions. May Allah (SWT) bestow upon his forgiveness to the entire ummah and ummah of all the Prophet s (AS). And all those who received the right guidance.

The purpose of the book is to examine the information strategy of the Prophet (ﷺ). It includes collection, processing, and dissemination of information for decision making. The Prophet (ﷺ) used to collect information from human resources which was the prevalent means of the subject. However, we understand that he was also receiving Devine revelation. It was an extraordinary source of information, nevertheless, we have examined the physical sources of information. The processing did not develop as it is today, therefore, it does not occupy a big slice in the book. The dissemination was direct to the decision makers either to him or any other target.

The author had investigated five instances or case studies: the conquest of Makkah, the battle of Hunain, The treaty of Hodhbia, the Tabuk expedition and the Hijrah expedition. Some provide detailed account of the subject, and some describe the issue briefly.

I pray to Allah (SWT), the Exalted, to accept the humble effort and make it a source of forgiveness for me and the entire ummah. May it be a source of guidance for readers. Ameen!

The author welcomes any suggestions to incorporate them in the future editions.

Prof Javed Iqbal Saani, Ph.D.
Manchester 20 November 2019

1 INTRODUCTION TO INFORMATION MANAGEMENT

Introduction

Information management is concerned with capturing, processing, and conveying information at right and right contents. Managers make important decisions with the information provided to them. Timely and correct information enable them to make informed decisions to achieve their goals. This chapter investigates a generic approach of the Prophet (ﷺ) while rest of the book examines specific cases.

A-Methods of capturing information

There are a few instances of capturing information; they are described here in turn. The Prophet had used various approached for the purpose; five instances are here for our understanding. But it is not an exhaustive list of the methods applied.

1- Scouting before the battle of Badr

Mubarikpuri reports "In the immediate vicinity of Badr, the Prophet (ﷺ) and his cave mate Abu Bakr (RA) conducted a scouting operation during which they managed to locate the camp of Quraish. They came across an old Bedouin nearby ... and managed to extract from him the exact location of the army of the polytheists. In the evening of the same day, he (The Prophet (ﷺ)) despatched three Emigrant leaders, Ali bin Abi Talib, Az-Zubair bin Al-'Awwam and Sa'd bin Abi Waqqas to scout about for news about the enemy. They saw two men drawing water for the Makkan army. On interrogation, they admitted that they were water carriers working for Quraish. But that answer did not please some Muslims and they beat the two boys severely to exact from them an answer, even if it is not true, alluding to the caravan laden with wealth. The two boys thus lied, and so they were released. The Prophet (ﷺ) was angry with those men and censured them saying: "On telling the truth, you beat them, and on telling a lie, you released them!" He then addressed the two boys and after a little conversation with them he learned a lot about the enemy: number of soldiers, their exact location, and names of some of their notables."[1]

2-Catching the enemy spy

According to Lings, "For several days nothing was achieved; but on the sixth night, when 'Umar was in command of the watch, a spy was caught in the camp, and in return for his life he gave them valuable information about the various fortresses, telling them which they could capture most easily and suggesting that they should begin with one which was not well guarded and which had a quantity of weapons stored in its spacious cellars, including

---

[1] Mubarikpuri, p. 215.

some engines of war that had been used in the past against other fortresses, for like Yathrib Khaybar had often been plagued with civil discord." 2

Impact of information
Lings states "The next day the fortress was taken, and the engines brought out to be used in other assaults, a ballista for hurling rocks and two testudos for bringing men up to the walls beneath an impregnable roof so that they could breach an entrance." 3

3- Sending a companion

The Messenger of God said to one of his companions, "Say, 'Yes, it is a rendezvous between us and you.'" Then the Messenger of God sent 'Ali b. Abi Talib, saying, "Go out following in the tracks of the enemy, and see what they are doing and what they intend doing. If they are leading their horses and riding their camels, they are making for Mecca, but if they are riding their horses and leading their camels, they are making for Medina. By the one who has my soul in his hands, if they are making for Medina, I shall go to them there and take the field against them!"4

Lings reports the account in detail. "the Prophet (ﷺ) sent Sa'd of Zuhrah down to the plain to follow them and see what they were about. "If they are leading their horses", he said, "and riding their camels, they are for Mecca; but if they are riding their horses and leading their camels, they

---

2 Lings, p. 265-66.

3 Lings, p. 266.

4 Tabari, V. 7, p. 132.

are for Medina; and by Him in whose hand is my soul, if that is their aim, I will overtake them and fight them." Sa'd went down to the gully where the Prophet's (ﷺ) stallion Sakb had been tethered ever since their arrival in Hedland having ridden after the Meccans until he had a clear sight of them, heathen hastened back with the good tidings that their horsemen were on camelback leading their horses beside them."[5]

4- Deputing a soldier

The Prophet (ﷺ) sent one of his companions to enquire about the movements of enemy. Lings says "As soon as Hudhaifah had heard the order to march he made his way to the camp of Ghatafan, but found the place deserted, for the wind had broken their resistance also and they were already on their way to Najd, So he returned to the Prophet (ﷺ), who was standing in prayer, cloaked against the cold in a wrapper belonging to one of his wives. "When he saw me," said Hudhaifah, "he motioned me to sit beside him at his feet and threw the end of the wrapper over me. Then, with me still in it, he made the bowing and the prostrations. When he had uttered the final greeting of peace, I told him the news.[6]

5-Through the intelligence personnel

Mubarikpuri reports that before the small expedition of Dhi Amr; "The Prophet's (ﷺ) intelligence personnel reported that Banu Tha'labah and Banu Muharib were mustering troops with the aim of raiding the outskirts of

---

[5] Lings, p. 190.

[6] Lings, p. 228.

Madinah. The Prophet (ﷺ) at the head of 450 horsemen, and footmen set out to handle this new situation. 'Uthman bin 'Affan was asked to dispose the affairs of the Muslims in Madinah."⁷

B-Methods of dissiminating information

The Prophet (ﷺ) had sent many invitation letters to various heads of states/governors etc. around the peninsula. However, he used to send people to issue information. For instance, the Prophet (ﷺ) used to distribute revelation as soon as he received them. When Umar (RA) went to his sister house before accepting Islam. They had a part of the scripture, "and he was with them at that moment with some written pages of Ta-Ha which had just been revealed and which they were reading together."⁸

1- Umar (RA) for lifting the siege of Ta'if

When the Prophet (ﷺ) wanted to *lift the siege of Taif*, he sent "Umar bin Al-Khattab, who was ordered by the Prophet (ﷺ) to notify people, said to them "If Allah (SWT) will, we are leaving the castle and going back tomorrow."⁹

2-Two envoys for the news of victory of Badr

The news of victory of Badr. According to Lings "As soon as it became clear that the eight hundred or more Meccan troops still at large had been routed beyond possibility of rallying, the Prophet (ﷺ) sent Abd Allah ibn Rawahah to

---

⁷ Mubarikpuri, p. 240.

⁸ Lings, p. 86.

⁹ Mubarikpuri, p. 410.

take the good tidings of victory to the people of Upper Medina, that is, the more southerly part of the city, and he sent Zayd (RA) to the people of Lower Medina."[10]

3-Deputation of key personnel to answer Abu Syufyan

Abu Syufyan was boosting for some upper hand he had in the battlefield after the expedition of Uhad, "The Prophet(ﷺ) told 'Umar to go and answer him, saying: "God is All Highest, Supreme in Majesty. We are not equal: our slain are in Paradise, yours are in the Fire." So 'Umar went to the edge of the precipice below which Abu Sufyan was standing and answered him as the Prophet (ﷺ) had said."[11]

4-Ali (RA) as special representative

When ayaat revealed about the pagans etc. to prohibit them from entry in the holy sanctuary. "The Messenger of God (ﷺ) sent 'Ali (RA) b. Abi Talib immediately after Abu Bakr (RA) had left. He overtook him at al-'Arj, and ('Ali (RA)) read the declaration of dispensation (al-Bara'ah) on the day of sacrifice at al-'Aqabah.[12] "He was to recite the revealed verses in the valley of Mina and he was also to make it clear that no one after that year would be allowed to go round the Holy House naked, and that idolaters were making the Pilgrimage for the last time ... 'Ali proclaimed the Divine Message. The gist of it was that the idolaters were given four months 'respite to come and go as they pleased in

---

[10] Lings p. 151.

[11] Lings, p. 190.

[12] Tabari, V. 9, p. 78.

safety, but after that God and His Messenger (ﷺ) would be free from any obligation towards them. War was declared upon them, and they were to be slain or taken captive wherever they were found."[13]

5-Through letters

The Prophet (ﷺ) had sent many ambassadors to the heads of states to invite them towards Islam. The invitations were in black and white. Animal skin was also in use to write letters those days.

The Prophet (ﷺ) appointed Abdullah b. Jahsh for the Nakhlah campaign; according to Tabari "The Messenger of God (ﷺ) wrote him (i.e., 'Abd Allah b. Jahsh) a letter, but ordered him not to look at it until he had travelled for two days. Then he was to look at it and to carry out what he was commanded in it but not to compel any of his companions to do anything against their will. When 'Abd Allah b. Jahsh had travelled two days, he opened the letter and looked at it, and it said, "When you look at my letter, march until you halt at Nakhlah, between Mecca and al-Ta'if. Observe Quraysh there and find out for us what they are doing." When 'Abd Allah looked at the letter he said, "I heed and obey." Then he said to his companions, "The Messenger of God has commanded me to go to Nakhlah and observe Quraysh so that I can bring him news of them."[14]

C- Sources of information

They were Divine revelation and human resources. We describe some instances here.

---

[13] Lings, p. 323.

[14] Tabari, V. 7, p. 18.

Devine revelation

Since he was a Prophet (ﷺ), yet the primary source of information was the *revelation*. It includes the scripture and information about other instances. One incident was remarkably interesting about the acceptance of Islam of Umayr bin Wahab but his intention was different.

Kandhelvi states when Umayr bin Wahab arrived in Madinah for assassinating the Prophet (ﷺ) "Hadhrat Umar *(RA)* then came to Rasulullaah (ﷺ) and said, "*o* Nabi of Allaah! The enemy of Allaah Umayr bin Wahab has come with a sword hanging from his neck. Rasulullaah (ﷺ) said, "Allow him to meet me." Hadhrat Umar (RA) grabbed hold of the handle of Umayr bin Wahab's sword and pulled him towards Rasulullaah (ﷺ) by the collar. He then said to the men of the Ansaar who were with him, "Go to Rasulullaah (ﷺ) and sit with him. Watch this wretch closely for he cannot be trusted." He then brought Umayr bin Wahab to Rasulullaah (ﷺ) When Rasulullaah (ﷺ) saw him with Hadhrat Umar (RA) pulling him by the handle of his sword at his collar, Rasulullaah (ﷺ) said, "Leave him, *o* Umar! You may come closer, *o* Umayr." When Umayr bin Wahab came closer to Rasulullaah (ﷺ) he greeted with the words, "Blessed is your morning." This was the way people greeted during the Period of Ignorance. Rasulullaah (ﷺ) said, "Allaah has blessed us with a greeting better than your greeting, *o* Umayr. He has blessed us with the greeting of Salaam which is the greeting of the people of Jannah." 'Well," said Umayr, "By Allaah! This is new to me, *o* Muhammad." Rasulullaah (ﷺ) asked, 'What brings you here, *o* Umayr?" Umayr replied, "I have come regarding this prisoner that you have with you. Please be kind to him." Rasulullaah (ﷺ) asked, 'Why then the sword around your neck?" Umayr cursed, "These swords! Have they ever done us any good?!"*Rasulullaah (ﷺ) said, "Tell me the truth. What have you come for?" "I have come only for this," lied Umayr. Rasulullaah (ﷺ) then said to him, 'You and' Safwaan bin Umayyah were sitting in the Hateem and discussing what had happened to the people of the well when you said, 'Had it not been for my debts and the family I have, I would have gone to kill Muhammad' Safwaan then assumed responsibility for your debts and your family if you would kill me. However, Allaah stands between you and I."*[15] Thus the "Prophet (ﷺ) repeated to him word for word the conversation he had had in the Haram with Safwan, "So Safwan took upon himself thy debt and thy family," he concluded, "that thou shouldst slay me; but God hath come between thee and that." "Who told thee this," cried 'Umayr, "for by God there was no third man with us? "Gabriel told me," said the Prophet (ﷺ).[16]

Similarly, the recovery of a letter which a woman was carrying before the conquest of Makkah was possible through Devine information. Mubarikpuri states the incident as "There was so much dread and fear everywhere that Hatib, one of the most trusted followers of the Prophet (ﷺ) secretly despatched a female messenger with a letter to Makkah containing intimation of the intended attack. The Prophet (ﷺ) received news from the heaven of Hatib's action and sent Ali (RA) and Al-Miqdad (RA) with instructions to go after her. They overtook the messenger,

---

[15] Kandhelvi (2012), P.212.

[16] Lings, p. 158.

and after a long search discovered the letter carefully hidden in her locks."17

Deployment of personnel

The Prophet (ﷺ) had appointed his companions to keep an eye on the movements and activities of enemy. When Umar (RA) embraced Islam, he went to the mosque and asked one of the companions "O Khubab, said 'Umar, "where will Muhammad now be, that I may go to him and enter Islam?" Khubab told him that he was at the house of Arqam near the Safa Gate with many of his companions; and 'Umar girt on his sword again and went to Safa, knocked at the door of the house, and said who he was. They had been warned by Nu'aym, so that his coming was expected, but they were struck by the subdued tone of his voice."18

It suggests that the Prophet's (ﷺ) men were walking around the places, and they knew where the Prophet (ﷺ) was staying. They were capturing news and conveying to the Prophet (ﷺ). When Umar (RA) reached the house of Arqum (RA) for accepting Islam, the people in the home knew about his arrival.

However, the human was the principal sources of both information capturing and distribution. The Prophet (ﷺ) had used written sources as well.

Seeking secrecy of information

Security of information was especially important during the conquest of Makkah, hence the Prophet (ﷺ) made supplication for it "O God, take from Quraysh all sight of

---

17 Mubarikpuri, p. 390.

18 Lings p. 87.

us, and all tidings of us, what we are about, that we may come suddenly upon them in their land."[19]

The Prophet (ﷺ) also used to keep secret his destinations for military campaigns with a few exceptions. He said once "Narrated Jabir ibn Abdullah: The Prophet (ﷺ) said: Meetings are confidential except three: those for the purpose of shedding blood unlawfully, or committing fornication, or acquiring property unjustly."[20]

Methods of saving information

Since the paper was not in use for large scale projects yet other objects were used to write down scripture and other documents such as animal skin, bones etc. The Prophet (ﷺ) had memorised the holy Quran and there were others who did the same. Most of the information was in tacit form, in the memory of people.

---

[19] Lings, p. 292.

[20] Sunan Abi Dawud 4869.

2 CASE STUDY: THE CONQUEST OF MAKKAH

The brief account of the expedition

The cause of the expedition was the breach of contract of Hodhabia. Banu Khaza was the Confederate of Muslims while Banu Baker was the ally of Quraysh. They had enmity since long; the truce restricted both to initiative any venture against each other. But Banu Baker dared to attack Banu Khaza. Quraysh helped them with arms and secretly joined them for the killing of many people of the victims. The latter approached the Prophet (ﷺ) for help.

The prophet (ﷺ) sent an envoy to Quraysh to pay the blood money of the victims, to withdraw the support of Banu Baker or cancel the treaty of Hodhabia. Quraysh embraced the last condition in haste. The envoy conveyed the message to the prophet(ﷺ). It was augmented when the delegation of Khaza also approached the prophet (ﷺ) to explain the incident and solicit the help.

The prophet (ﷺ) was guided by the Divine power. He decided to take a decisive measure against long waiting decision against Quraysh. His decision eliminated the opposition of Lords of Makkah forever.

Preparation

Following the failed visit of Abu Sufyan for restoration of the treaty of Hodhabia the prophet (ﷺ) ordered for the preparation of the battle. He supplicated for the security of the campaign to avoid bloodshed. The prophet (ﷺ) also sent message to the Confederate tribes for joining him on the way to Makkah while keeping the news in camera. Kandhelvi notes,

Hadhrat Abdullaah bin Abbaas (RA) narrates that when Rasulullaah (ﷺ) left Madinah (for Makkah), he appointed Abu Ruhm Kulthoom bin Husayn Ghifaari (RA) as the Ameer of Madinah. He left on the tenth of Ramadhan while he and the Sahabah (RA) were fasting. They broke their fasts when they reached, Kudayd which was an oasis between Usfaan and Amj. Rasulullaah (ﷺ) then proceeded with the ten thousand Sahabah (RA) until they set up camp at Marruz Zahraan. There were also a thousand people from the Muzayna and Sulaym tribes and every tribe had brought provisions and weapons. Every one of the Muhaajireen and Ansaar left with Rasulullaah (ﷺ) without anyone remaining behind.[21]

Similarly, Lings says,

The Prophet (ﷺ) now sent messengers to those of the tribes whom he felt he could now rely on for help, with a general summons to be present in Medina at the beginning of the next month, which was Ramadan, The Bedouin faithfully responded; and when the appointed day came the army was the largest that had ever set out from Medina. No able-bodied Muslim stayed behind. The Emigrants were seven hundred, with three hundred horses; the Helpers were four thousand, with five hundred horses; and the tribes,

---

[21] P.179.

including those who joined them on the way, brought the total numbers up to ten thousand men. The cavalry rode on camelback, leading their horses.[22]

The Islamic army left Madhina in the beginning of Ramadan. Other joined them on the way to Makkah. It used to be a week's journey. People of the city were unaware of the movement because Allah, the exalted blocked all news. Nevertheless, Quraysh were expecting Muslims. It was also believed that the target could had been Hawazin Quraysh. But some close companions knew the real destination.

Muslim at the outstrips of the destination.
When the prophet (ﷺ) reached near Makkah, he stayed and asked his generals to light the lights so that Quraysh considered it a massive army. Lings drew the sketch in the following words,

The army halted at Dhu Tuwa, which is near to the city and within sight of it. This was the place where two years previously Khalid (RA) had been stationed bar their approach. But now there was no sign of any to resistance. It was as if the city were empty, as it had been at their visit the previous year. But this time there was no three-day limit to their stay; and when Qaswa' came to a halt the Prophet (ﷺ) bowed his head until his beard almost touched the saddle, in gratitude to God. He then drew up his troops, putting Khalid in command of the right and Zubayr in command of the left. His own troop which was now in the centre he divided into two; half of it was to be led by Sa'd and his son, and the other half, in which he himself would ride, was to be led by Abu 'Ubaydah, When the order was

---

[22] P. 293.

given they were to divide and to enter the city from four directions, Khalid from below and the others from the hills through three different passes.[23]

Abu Sufyan was in control of Quraysh. Abbas (RA) brought him to the prophet (ﷺ) who asked him to keep him in a tent and bring him the next day. It worked and Abu Sufyan becomes a Muslim.

The prophet (ﷺ) asked him to stay at a given place and watch the Islamic troops. The purpose was to realise him that it was impossible for Quraysh to dare to take the risk of an open fight. Kandhelvi (2012) describes the situation.

As Abu Sufyaan was leaving, Rasulullaah (ﷺ) said, "O Abbaas! Keep him in the valley at the point where the mountain protrudes so that he may witness the armies of Allaah marching by." Hadhrat Abbaas - says that in compliance with the instruction of Rasulullaah (ﷺ) he took Abu Sufyaan to the point where the valley narrowed.

The various tribes then began passing by him, each bearing their flags. When a tribe passed by, Abu Sufyaan asked, "who are they, o Abbaas (RA)?" "They are the Banu Sulaym tribe," came the reply. To this, Abu Sufyaan would say, "What have I to do with the Banu Sulaym (Why should they be marching against us)?" When another tribe passed, Abu Sufyaan asked, "Who are they, o Abbaas?" When Hadhrat Abbaas (RA) informed him that they were the Muzaynah tribe, Abu Sufyaan said, "What have I to do with the Muzaynah tribe?" This continued until all the tribes had passed. Each time a tribe passed, Abu Sufyaan would ask, "Who are they, o Abbaas?" When informed, Abu Sufyaan would say, "What have I to do with them?"

---

[23] P. 298.

Eventually, Rasulullaah (ﷺ) passed by with a large group that included the muh'aajireen and Ansaar. (Because of their armour and helmets) Nothing but the whites of their eyes were visible. Abu Sufyaan exclaimed, "Subhaanallaah! Who are they, o Abbaas!" "That," replied, Hadhrat Abbaas (RA) is Rasulullaah (ﷺ) with the Muhaajireen and the Ansaar." Abu Sufyaan said, "None has the power or capacity to resist them. o Abul Fadhl! I swear by Allaah! The empire of your nephew has certainly become enormous." Hadhrat Abbaas (RA) said, "o Abu Sufyaan! This is Nabuwaat (and not the average kingly empire)." Abu Sufyaan acknowledged this by saying, "Indeed, now that you mention it." Hadhrat Abbaas (RA) then said to him, "Go to your people (and inform them about what is happening)." Abu Sufyaan then left and came to the people of Makkah, shouting at the top of his voice, "o Quraysh! Muhammad is on his way with an army that you have no power to restrain. Whoever enters the house of Abu Sufyaan shall be safe." His wife Hind bint Utba stood before him and grabbed hold of his moustache saying, "Kill this dark wretch! He brings ill news!" Abu Sufyaan said, "Shame on you people! Do not let this woman mislead you because Rasulullaah (ﷺ) is certainly approaching with an army that you have no power to restrain. Whoever enters the house of Abu Sufyaan shall be safe."

The people said, "Shame on you! Your house shall never accommodate all of us." Abu Sufyaan then said, 'Whoever locks the door of his house shall be safe and whoever enters the Masjid shall be safe." The people then dispersed towards their homes and the Masjid.

Abu Sufyan observed the troops and concluded that it was not useful to counter the Islamic army. The prophet (ﷺ) offered him favourable terms to avoid an open conflict.

Islamic army took the control of Makkah

Therefore, the Islamic army took the control of the city without significant resistance. A band of "cleaver" Quraishes tried to challenged Khalid's (RA) battalion who put them one flight and left 30 dead bodies on ground. Two Muslims attained martyrdom in the encounter.[24]

The Prophet (ﷺ) announced general amnesty to the people of Makkah. Table 1 in chapter 3 summarizes the key action he had taken to forgive his opponents and established peace in the city.

The Prophet (ﷺ) cleaned the house of Allah (SWT) from the idols and prayed. He had handed over the key to Kaaba to the Usman bin Talha (RA) and confirmed the right of Quraysh to remain the guardian of pilgrims, managing drinking water etc.

The Prophet (ﷺ) also sent many small expeditions to destroy the symbol of idolatry. Mubarikpuri reports one of them as,

He sent Khalid bin Al-Waleed in Ramadan 8 A.H. to a spot called Nakhlah where there was a goddess called Al-'Uzza venerated by Quraish and Kinahan tribes. It had custodians from Bani Shaiban. Khalid, at the head of thirty horsemen arrived at the spot and exterminated it. On his return, the Prophet (ﷺ) asked him if he had seen anything there, to which Khalid gave a negative answer. Here, he was told that it had not been destroyed and he had to go there again and fulfil the task. He went back again and there he saw a black woman, naked with torn hair. Khalid struck her with his sword into two parts. He returned and narrated the story to

---

[24] Lings, p. 299.

the Prophet (ﷺ) who then confirmed the fulfilment of the task.

The Prophet (ﷺ) stayed about three weeks in the city meanwhile the battle of Honain took place because the Hawazin assembled in the nearby area to challenge Muslims. The Prophet (ﷺ) left for the expedition.

The information strategy

One of the distinguishing features of the conquest of Makkah was the secrecy of information the prophet (ﷺ) had kept on the occasion. We know the science of information management involves gathering, processing and dissemination of information for marking informed decisions. We will take these elements in turn.

We understand that the purpose of the book is to investigate the managerial implications of the event as understood today. Information management is one of the topics.

Collecting information

The purpose of information gathering was to keep an eye on the honouring of the treaty of Hodhabia. The Muslims also wanted to keep informed about the common activities of Quraysh in connection with peace and security. The treaty provided the basis of peace of mind from the enemy, but it was vulnerable. Therefore, the prophet (ﷺ) must keep himself informed about the activities of Quraysh. The first piece of information was the written agreement of the treaty of Hodhabia. The second piece of information was the confederation of the Muslims and Banu Khaza after the treaty of Hodhabia. The third piece of information was the news that Banu

Baker attacked on Banu Khaza. The former was an ally of Quraysh.

The fourth piece of information was the arrival of the delegation of the affected tribe in Madhina. He was Amr bin Salim of Khaza. Haykal writes,

After running in full haste toward Madinah, `Amr ibn Salim al Khuza'i related to Muhammad and the Muslims in the mosque what had happened and asked for assistance. The Prophet (ﷺ) of God answered "Certainly, o `Amr ibn Salim, we shall come to your rescue." Another group of Khuza'ah tribe members followed him to Madinah together with their Makkan host, Budayl ibn Warqa', and confirmed their predecessor's report.25

Processing information

It involves converting data into information as it is prevalent today. We understand that data is the raw facts while information is the meaningful facts. The act of converting data into information is called the process of conversion. It is the process of screening facts from one stage to the other.
If we analyse the above quotations from data and information, we can say that the information was the attack of Banu Baker to Banu Khaza. The remaining text was data. However, the process of conversion or screening was a mental activity. It takes place in the minds of both the recipient and the transmitter. Thus, the processing power

---

25 Muhammad Husayn Haykal, Translated by Isma'il Razi A. al-Faruqi, The Life of Muhammad (ﷺ)

http://www.witness-pioneer.org/vil/Books/MH_LM/default.htm

was the human minds as opposed to the computers. They were also the storage devices. Nevertheless, the information was also recorded in writing form. For example, the names of the soldiers used to be recorded in registers.

Storage mechanism
We know that electronic devices and data storage were not available but other traditional instruments were there. Leather skins, leaves of trees etc. were used for recording of Quran. It enabled Usman (RA) to compile the manuscript. The same objects were used for record keeping at the time of the conquest of Makkah.

Dissemination
The common approach was the application of human resources. Special envoys were sent to convey messages. Many examples appeared during the event. The delegation of Khaza came to inform the prophet (ﷺ) about the invasion of Banu Baker. The prophet (ﷺ) sent an envoy to Quraysh about the breach of the treaty who put forward the conditions of resolution or restoration of the treaty. In addition, Abu Sufyan came to the Prophet (ﷺ) to revive the treaty of Hodhabia. Mubarikpuri writes about it, he says, Quraysh "at once called for an emergency meeting and decided to delegate their chief Abu Sufyan to Madinah for a renewal of the truce. He directly headed for the house of his daughter Umm Habiba (the Prophet's(ﷺ) wife)."[26]
Written messages were also in use. One of the companions sent a letter to Quraysh to inform them about the intention

---

[26] P. 390.

of the prophet(ﷺ). Because his family was in Makkah and no one was there to offer them protection in case of a battle.

Secrecy of information

Although secrecy is one of the critical success factors in any military campaign, it was kept as a special element in the battle. We have examined it in this section. The purpose of secrecy was to reach the head of the enemy suddenly so that he could not yet prepare for the combat. It makes things easy to overcome the opposition. The prophet (ﷺ) wanted to minimize casualties. His strategy was successful because the aims were conducted with minimum human loss. The infidels challenged the battalion of Khalid bin Waleed and picked up two dozen dead bodies.

Alternative view

Mubarikpuri, one of the famous biographers of the prophet (ﷺ) writes that the prophet (ﷺ) had announced the destination after the visit of Abu Sufyan. In other words, the target was Quraysh.[27] However, Lings, another famous writer on the subject believes that it could be people of Taif i.e. Hawazin. He writes,

The Prophet (ﷺ) himself and many others fasted until they were within a certain distance of the sacred territory; then he gave orders to break the fast; and when they had encamped at Marr az-Zahran he let it be known that the reason for breaking the fast had been to gather up their strength for meeting the enemy. This aroused the curiosity of some of the men to breaking point. From Marr az-

---

[27] P. 540.

Zahran, Mecca could be reached in one long day's march, and easily in two. But in view of the truce, it was unlikely that they had come out against Quraysh. Their camp was also on the way to the territory of the hostile tribes of Hawazin. Or could it be that having gained possession of the northern garden of the Hijaz, the Prophet (ﷺ) was now bent on capturing its southern garden, the hitherto impregnable Ta'if, the centre of the worship of al-Lat?[28]

The prophet (ﷺ) was stationed about two days journey from where either of the targets could be reached i.e., Quraysh or Hawazin. Many people were curious about the target. In the words of Lings,

"Who are the enemy?" was being passed from man to man throughout the host, Ka'b ibn Malik volunteered to go to the Prophet (ﷺ) and ask him. He did not, however, venture to put the question directly, but going to where the Prophet(ﷺ) was seated outside his tent he knelt in front of him and recited four melodious verses he had just composed for the occasion. The gist of these was that the men had reached the point of drawing their swords and interrogating them as to what enemy their edges were destined for, and that if the swords could have spoken, they too would have put the same question. But the Prophet's (ﷺ) only answer was a smile, and Ka'b had to return to the men with nothing achieved.[29]

However, he also mentioned that "The Prophet (ﷺ) now sent messengers to those of the tribes whom he felt he could now rely on for help, with a general summons to be present in Medina at the beginning of the next month, which was

---

[28] P. 294.

[29] P. 294-95.

Ramadan, The Bedouin faithfully responded; and when the appointed day came the army was the largest that had ever set out from Medina. No able-bodied Muslim stayed behind. The Emigrants were seven hundred, with three hundred horses; the Helpers were four thousand, with five hundred horses; and the tribes, including those who joined them on the way, brought the total numbers up to ten thousand men. The cavalry rode on camelback, leading their horses; and except for a few of the closest Companions none of them knew who the enemy were."[30]

Deputation of a small squadron

The prophet (ﷺ) had sent a small team to the area called Baton Azum. The purpose was to show that the prophet (ﷺ) intended to focus on the people of Baton. And the squad was the advanced party. The news was given as such. The team reached the area but was called back to join the prophet (ﷺ) for the campaign.[31]

The above instances suggest the level of security of information he had kept.

The Devine help

One of the true companions of the prophet (ﷺ) had his family in Makkah. He though a fierce fight between Quraysh and the Muslims because the former was famous for their bravery and determination. They dared to attack thrice to Muslims despite a decisive defeat in the first episode. He wanted to inform Quraysh about the situation

---

[30] P. 293.

[31] Mubarikpuri, p. 541.

in Madhina to save his family. Haykal provides the details. He writes,

While the Muslim army prepared to leave Madinah, Hatib ibn Abu Balta'ah wrote a letter informing the Quraysh about the Muslim move and gave it to a woman called Sarah, a client of some members of the house of Banu `Abd al Muttalib. He commanded her to take it to Makkah and to hand it over to the Quraysh leaders. Hatib was one of the foremost Muslims. How then could he now turn informant for the enemy? There are sides of the human soul which remain weak despite the great strength achieved by other sides, and man stays forever at the mercy of his weaknesses despite his conscious effort to overcome them. At any rate, Muhammad, soon learned of Hatib's attempt and sent `Ali ibn Abu Talib and al Zubayr ibn al `Awwam to intercept the messenger. The latter was arrested, and her horse and saddle searched, but no letter was found. `Ali threatened her that unless she produced the letter voluntarily, he would be forced to search her own person and to unveil her body in the process. When the woman realized how serious `Ali was, she loosened her pigtails, brought out the letter and handed it over to `Ali. The woman was returned to Madinah.[32] The Devine help kept the secrecy the Prophet (ﷺ) Wanted to keep.

---

[32] P. 428.

3 CASE STUDY: THE BATTLE OF HUNAIN

The brief account of the battle

The Hunain was adjunct battle with the conquest of Mecca. Although most of the tribes living around Mecca were defeated psychologically and they accepted it. Nevertheless, some big tribes did not embrace the superiority of Muslims. They dared to fight with the power. Notable tribes were Howzaan and Sakeef; they had also seduced some others as well. They formed a united army; the total number of the united forces were about 4000. the Muslims were 12000 including 2000 of the Muslims from Mecca and surroundings. The opponents were so dare that they travelled from various parts of the area and gathered near Makkah, the newly conquered city of Muslims. They forgot that the moral of the Muslim army was extremely high because they were victorious against the most powerful (or it was perceived as such) stratum of the area. And they had outnumbered them as well. One of the old men and an expert of war warned the leader about his war strategy but he rejected the words of wisdom. It became costly and he had paid the price. The leader was also doubtful about the outcome of the battle. He was unsure about the ability or loyalty of participants. Therefore, he tried to force his troops to fight or die. He implemented the famous military slogan "do or die".

Muslims advance

The Prophet (ﷺ) received the news of enemy and prepared his Army for the encounter. He borrowed some weapons, appointed the deputy in Makkah and moved towards Hunain, the possible place for the battle. The enemy already captured the place of battle, therefore, as soon as the Islamic Army entered the place the enemy showered the arrows upon them. It caused stampede in the Islamic troops initially but later they gathered again on the call of the Prophet (ﷺ) and fought fiercely. The Prophet (ﷺ) threw a handful of sand towards the enemy which reached in the eyes of every soldier. They were rubbing their eyes and the Muslim army started to slaughter them.

It is reported in the following hadith,

It has been narrated on the authority of 'Abbas who said: I was in the company of the Messenger of Allah (ﷺ) on the Day of Hunain. I and Abd Sufyan b. Harith b. 'Abd al-Muttalib stuck to the Messenger of Allah (ﷺ), and we did not separate from him. And the Messenger of Allah (may place be upon him) was riding on his white mule which had been presented to him by Farwa b. Nufitha al-Judhami. When the Muslims had an encounter with the disbelievers, the Muslims fled, falling back, but the Messenger of Allah (ﷺ) began to spur his mule towards the disbelievers. I was holding the bridle of the mule of the Messenger of Allah (ﷺ) checking it from going extremely fast, and Abu Sufyan was holding the stirrup of the (mule of the) Messenger of Allah (ﷺ), who said: Abbas, call out to the people of al-Samura. Abbas (who was a man with a loud voice) called out at the top of the voice: Where is the people of Samura? (Abbas said:) And by God, when they heard my voice, they came back (to us) as cows come back to their calves, and said: We are present, we are present! 'Abbas said: They began to fight the infidels. Then there was a call to The Ansar. Those (who called out to them) shouted: O ye party of the Ansar! O party of the Ansar! Banu al-Harith b. al-Khazraj were the last to be called. Those (who called out to them) shouted: O Banu Al-Harith b. al-Khazraj! O Banu Harith b. al-Khazraj! And the Messenger of Allah (ﷺ) who was riding on his mule looked at their fight with his neck stretched forward and he said: This is the time when the fight is raging hot. Then the Messenger of Allah (ﷺ) took (some) pebbles and threw them in the face of the infidels. Then he said: By the Lord of Muhammad, the infidels are defeated. 'Abbas said: I went around and saw that the battle was in the same condition in which I had seen it. By Allah (SWT), it remained in the same condition until he threw the pebbles. I continued to watch until I found that their force had been spent out and they began to retreat. [Sahih Muslim: Book 32, Hadith 94]

The enemy left 70 bodies in the battlefield. Muslims captured many captives and animals were in addition to the casualties.

Muslims won the day.

Consequently, the Muslims won the day; the enemy was defeated and their soldiers took flight towards three different directions. The first one went towards Nakhlah, another went towards Taif and the third one flew towards Otaas. The details have been described here as,

Abu Burda reported on the authority of his father that when Allah's (SWT) Apostle (ﷺ) had been free from the Battle of Hunain, he sent Abu 'Amir as the head of the army of Autas. He had an encounter with Duraid b. as_Simma. Duraid was killed and Allah (SWT) gave defeat to his friends. Abu Musa said:

He (the Holy Prophet) sent me along with Abu 'Amir and Abu 'Amir received a wound in his knee from the arrow, (shot by) a person of Bani Jusham. It stuck in his knee. I went to him and said: Uncle, who shot an arrow upon you? Abu 'Amir pointed out to Abu Musa and said: Verily that one who shot an arrow upon me, in fact, killed me. Abu Musa said: I followed him with the determination to kill him and overtook him and when he saw me, he turned upon his heels. I followed him and I said to him: Don't you feel ashamed (that you run), aren't you an Arab? Why don't you stop? He stopped and I had an encounter with him, and we exchanged the strokes of (swords). I struck him with the sword and killed him. Then I came back to Abu Amir and said: Verily Allah (SWT) has killed the one who killed you. And he said: Now draw out this arrow. I drew out the arrow and there came out from that (wound) water. Abu 'Amir said: My nephew, go to Allah's (SWT) Messenger (ﷺ) and convey my greetings to him and tell him that Abu Amir begs you to ask forgiveness for him. And Abu Amir appointed me as the chief of the people, and he died after a brief time. When I came to Allah's (SWT) Apostle (ﷺ) I visited him, and he had been lying on the cot woven by strings and there was (no) bed over it and so there had been marks of the strings on the back of Allah's (SWT) Messenger (ﷺ) and on his sides. I narrated to him what had happened to us, narrated to him about Abu Amir, and said to him that he had made a request to the effect that forgiveness should be sought for him (from Allah (SWT)). Thereupon Allah's (SWT) Messenger (may peace be. upon him) called for water and performed ablution with it. He then lifted his hands and spoke. O Allah (SWT), grant pardon to Thy servant Abu Amir. (The Prophet had raised his hands so high for supplication) that I saw the whiteness of his armpits. He again said: O Allah (SWT), grant him distinction amongst most of Thine created beings or from amongst the people. I said: Allah's (SWT) Messenger, ask forgiveness for me too. Thereupon Allah's (SWT) Apostle (ﷺ) said: Allah (SWT), forgive the sins of Abdullah b. Qais (Abu Musa Ash'ari) and admit him to an elevated place on the Day of Resurrection. Abu Burda said: One prayer is for Abu 'Amir and the other is tor, Abu Musa. [Sahih Muslim: Book 44, Hadith 237]

The largest group took shelter in the castle. the Prophet (ﷺ) decided to follow them and siege the enemy. It took more than 20 days without any positive outcome. Therefore, the Prophet (ﷺ) withdrew his army. The Prophet (ﷺ) left the booty in Jeeranah before advancing to Taif. He returned to Jeeranah and distributed the booty.

Concerns of Ansar

There was some disappointment among the helpers regarding the distribution of booty; the Prophet (ﷺ) had addressed them and said I have distributed the booty to win the hearts of new Muslims. I understand that it creates some disappointment among the Helpers but he said people are taking only material and you are taking the Prophet (ﷺ) with you. Upon this everybody was happy, and the matter was resolved amicably.

However, after some days a delegation of Hozaan came after embracing Islam. They reclaimed their families so the Prophet (ﷺ) had managed to return their women and children. They were incredibly happy for this treatment and returned to their homes contentedly. The Prophet (ﷺ) did Umrah and return to Madinah as stated in the following hadith,

Narrated Anas: Allah's (SWT) Messenger (ﷺ) performed four `Umras, all in the month of Dhul-Qa'da, except the one which he performed with his Hajj (i.e. in Dhul-Hijja). He performed one `Umra from Al-Hudaibiya in Dhul-Qa'da, another `Umra in the following year in Dhul Qa'da a third from Al-Jirana where he distributed the war booty of Hunain, in Dhul Qa'da, and the fourth `Umra he performed was with his Hajj. [Sahih al-Bukhari: Book 64, Hadith 192]

Four major themes have been identified in the expedition. The Prophet (ﷺ) motivated his Troops many times which helped them to overcome the enemy. We will discuss it in a separate chapter. Similarly, the Prophet (ﷺ) had managed information effectively and efficiently; we are also dealing with the topic in a full chapter length. The Prophet (ﷺ) had made many decisions which are discussed in a separate chapter as well. Finally, the prophet (ﷺ) had financed the campaign with some added resources.

The information strategy

Information is the basis of decision making in every situation a manager encounter. There are dedicated department in the contemporary organisations for it. Information systems, decision support systems, and executive information systems have been established for the purpose. Although there were no such details at the time of the prophet (ﷺ), yet the importance of information and its management was as significant as it is today. This chapter extracts the information management strategy of the Prophet (ﷺ) as applied in the battle.

Capturing Information

The information strategy of the Prophet (ﷺ) during this battle was different. He used to send spies to gather information and convey to him. But the Prophet (ﷺ) had sent Abu Hadhadh Aslami (RA) to stay with the enemy and examine their activities in detail. He acted accordingly and convey the required information to him. It made easy for the Prophet (ﷺ) to make right decision.

The Prophet (ﷺ) had captured information about the intention of tribes living in the surrounding of Makkah. Most of the tribes accepted the supremacy of Muslims but some diehard wanted to resist. Hozaan and Sakeef were in front line. The Prophet (ﷺ) received information about their programme. The enemy joined their hands and marched towards Makkah where the Prophet (ﷺ) was staying since last 19 days after the conquest of the city. The Prophet (ﷺ) was informed that the opponents had brought women, children, and animals to pressurise participants. They must fight with all means to defend them in addition to protect tribal values. In other words, they could not imagine the possibility of defeat. It boosted their moral for the achievement of their objectives.

The Prophet (ﷺ) also received the news that the enemy commander was very emotional; he had rejected the wise suggestions of an old man who was highly experienced in the war strategy. When unnecessary emotions erupt in the minds, they overtake wisdom. The same happened to the opponents. They also forgot that they were fighting against a victorious army whose moral were high. And they were facing the Prophet (ﷺ) of Allah (SWT). But all the odds were overshadowed in the heat of foolishness.

Spies of the enemy

The enemy sent spies to investigate the condition of Muslims. These people had seen the angels as they had described them. They were feeling very tired and disappointed. When the commander asked them about it, they said we had seen some horse riders and after that our condition changed. In other words, they were feeling the strength of the Muslims and conveyed the message that it is difficult to fight with Muslims.

The Prophet (ﷺ) had kept an in eye on the enemy movement. When the Prophet (ﷺ) moved towards Hunain; one of the horse riders informed him the whereabout of the enemy. He said it looks like that the whole of the tribe had arrived including their women, children, and animals.

The Prophet (ﷺ) observed the enemy on flight at the closing movements of the battle. They ran away in three different directions. The first one flew towards Nakhlah, the second one took their way towards Otass. The third one took refuge in their hometown Taif.

Observation

The Prophet (ﷺ) was collecting information through his informants. On the of battle when the army scattered due to the stampede. The Prophet (ﷺ) observed the situation and shouted, 'O! people, come towards me I am the son of Abdullah."

Similarly, when the battle started fiercely the Prophet (ﷺ) observed the battlefield and said, the stove is heated now. It means that fight was at its peak now.

Dissemination of information

For the dissemination of information, the Prophet (ﷺ) had ordered his uncle Abbas whose voice was very high to inform people about myself i.e. that he was at a place. He shouted at top of his voice, where are the people of tree (referring to the Baitul-Rizwan) and where are the Helpers?

Record keeping.
As we have seen that Prophet (ﷺ) had appointed Masood bin Umar Ghaffari (RA) to look after the booty which was in large number. Record was maintained of the booty so that it could be distributed accordingly. On the way back from Taif the Prophet (ﷺ) had distributed it among the new Muslims and the participants of the battle.

The preference was given to the new Muslims for their motivation. Table 1 shows the details of the distribution.

Table 1 The details of the booty		
Name	Quantity	Cash
Abu Syufyan bin Harb (RA)	200 Camels	40 Okia (About 6 kg silver)
Yazeed bin Abu Sufyan (RA)	200 Camels	40 Okia (About 6 kg silver)
Maaviya bin Abu Sufyan (RA)	200 Camels	40 Okia (About 6 kg silver)
Hakeem bin Hazzaam	200 Camels	
Safwaan bin Ummiya (RA)	300 Camels	
Haris bin Kaldhah (RA)	100 Camels	

Some Quraysh and non-Quraysh leaders were also given 100 camels; some people were rewarded 50 camels and others 40 camels each.

After that, the Prophet (ﷺ) ordered one of the companions to count the remaining booty and the number of participants to estimate the individual allowance of the soldiers. Each soldier received four camels and forty goats. The horse riders were given three times more than the soldiers.

The Prophet (ﷺ) had also kept an eye on the developments among the participants; for instance, the most of the booty was distributed among the new Muslims and others but nothing was given to the helpers, therefore, there was some disappointment amongst them. The Prophet (ﷺ) came to know about it. He called a meeting of ansar/helpers and said I have received some complaints about the distribution of booty. He continued O! people of Ansar when I came to you, you were deprived of Islam, Allah (SWT) had given guidance to you through me; you were poor, Allah (SWT) had made you rich; you were enemy of each other, Allah (SWT) had made you friends of each other. All of them replied no doubt it was the grace of Allah (SWT) and his Prophet (ﷺ).

In response, the Prophet (ﷺ) said but if you want to say and you would say truth that O! Prophet (ﷺ) of Allah (SWT) you came to us when your nation refused to accept your message; we testified your message; you were let alone and helpless, we helped you; you were exiled, we had offered you a shelter. You were disappointed, we had shared your worries. The Prophet (ﷺ) informed them I have distributed booty for the motivation of people because there were new Muslims.

The purpose was to stabilize them on Islam. If there would be no migration, I would be staying with the Helpers. O! Helpers, people are taking material and animals today to their homes and you are taking the Prophet (ﷺ) with you. Are you not happy for that? They replied we want to take you, O! Prophet (ﷺ) of Allah (SWT). The people were happy after the address and scattered happily.

The Prophet (ﷺ) had intentionally delayed the distribution of booty because he was expecting the people of Taif to come and claim their families and animals. But they could not come on time, therefore, the Prophet (ﷺ) had distributed the booty. At last, they came. It has been reported that 14 of them became Muslims and approached the Prophet (ﷺ). They requested return of their families and animals. The Prophet (ﷺ) addressed the crowd and motivated them to return the spoil of war. In response after some hesitation, all the spoils of war were returned to them. The Hoazanion delegation was happy for such a cordial treatment from the Prophet (ﷺ) and the Muslims.

4 CASE STUDY: THE TABUK COMPAIGN

The brief account the compaign

We understand that this is one of the expeditions which took 50 days to complete. The popularity of muslins in the Arab peninsula was threatening big powers of the time: The Romans and the Persians. The former was gathering its troops to ruin Madinah. Prophet responded sternly. Announcements were made to the public about the long journey to be taken towards Tabuk, Northern Hajaaz. The weather was extremely hot, and the annual harvesting was drawing near. But more than 30,000 sahabah got ready to teach a lesson to the enemy. It took the army about a month to reach the envisioned destination. Financing considerable number of troops was a key question. Hazrat Usman (RA) contributed for one third of the entire brigade. Others also contributed generously; even than the necessities were scared not to speak of weapons. One camel was available for ten personnel. But the obedient followers were ready to do anything for the cause of faith. In fact, for Allah (SWT) and His prophet (ﷺ); for His pleasure. The prophet (ﷺ) stayed at the spot for a month or so, but the enemy could not dare to turn up. The Islamic army returned safely. The expedition sent a strong message across the world especially to the 'big brothers' to be vigilant because a new superpower was emerging. And it really happened after a couple of years when 'big brothers' were defeated and expelled from the Arab lands. The Islamic flag was flying over most of Asia and Africa.

Background

The enmity emerged with Romans when they martyred the Muslim envoy Hazrat Haris bin Umair Azri (RA). In response, the Prophet (ﷺ) had sent a small contingent under the command of Zaid bin Harsa (RA) who fought with the battle of Mota. However, the strength of the opponents was still considerable.

The immediate reason of this battle was the threat of Romans to invade Madinah. Also, after the defeat of Quraysh most of the Arab tribes where in favour of the Muslims. New tribes were entering in the fold of Islam and other tribes were considering embracing the new religion. Mubarikpuri states the worry of Byzantine Empire,

Caesar — who could neither ignore the great benefit the Mu'tah Battle had brought to Muslims, nor could he disregard the Arab tribes' expectations of independence, and their hopes of getting free from his influence and reign, nor he could ignore their alliance to the Muslims — realizing all that, Caesar was aware of the progressive danger threatening his borders, especially Ash-Sham-fronts which were neighbouring Arab lands. So, he concluded that demolition of the Muslims power had grown an urgent necessity. This decision of his should be achieved before the Muslims become too powerful to conquer and raise troubles and unrest in the adjacent Arab territories.33

To materialise these ambitions the Byzantines decided to initiate a decisive step to neutralise Muslim power. They gathered a large army with the help of their Arab confederates. At one point the enemy gathered 40,000 strong army and gathered in Belqa. It ignited the hopes of hypocrites of Madinah and surroundings. They wanted to eliminate Muslims as soon as possible at any cost. Therefore, they had constructed a separate place of worship so that they can conspire in privacy. It provided them a base camp for planning their malicious aspires. They were so much dare that they had invited the Prophet (ﷺ) to lead a prayer in the new place. The Prophet (ﷺ) postponed it till his return from the campaign.

The purpose of the Battle was to show Romans and others that Muslims were now a real military power in the area. The Battle would have completed the influence of Muslims in Arab lands; it was also a decent effort to control the hypocrites and others indeed.

Preparations

The Prophet (ﷺ) had recruited the companion from Medina, Arab tribes, and Makkah. In addition to the manpower, the Prophet (ﷺ) had contributed a lot of money and resources from Muslims to finance the army. He had appointed a deputy (Governor of Madinah) and deputed Ali (RA) for looking after his family. An enormous number of people gathered to accompany the Prophet (ﷺ).

---

33 P. 579.

On ground, the physical circumstances were very odd. It was hot, people were threatened with famine and poverty, mounts were limited, the crops were ready and the journey was long. It restricted people to go immediately for the campaign.

Nevertheless, the Prophet (ﷺ) had taken a decisive decision to go out at all costs. He knew that the invasion of Byzantines would create bad image of Muslims, they could lose the advantages of the previous conquests. The possibility of revival of idolaters could not be ruled out.

As a result, the Prophet (ﷺ) had announced the expedition. He invited people of Makkah, the confederate tribes, and the inhabitants of Madinah. He inspired people for fighting for the cause of Allah (SWT) and motivated them for spending in the path of Almighty. The companions had contributed generously but there was lack of resources due to the substantial number of participants. Many willing to join the campaign could not accompany the troops because of unavailability of mounts. Usman (RA), Abdurrehman bin Ouff (RA), Abu Bakr (RA), Umer (RA), Abbass (RA), Talha (RA), Saad bin Ubaidhah (RA), Muhammad bin Musalmah (RA), Asim bin Addi (RA) were the prominent contributors. Women also took part enthusiastically in the collection.

Passionate tribes and people gathered quickly on the call of the Prophet (ﷺ). Lings described the movements.

When all the Bedouin contingents had arrived, the army was thirty thousand strong, with ten thousand horses. A camp was made outside the town, and Abu Bakr was put in charge of it until, when all was ready for the march, the Prophet (ﷺ) himself rode forth and took command.[34]

The expedition and its impacts

It took him fifteen days to reach the destination. The Romans could not dare to face Muslims. The Prophet (ﷺ) stayed twenty days in the area and send many expeditions for conquering adjunct areas. Khalidh bin Waleedh (RA) was sent to Dhuma-tul_Jandhal with more than four hundred soldiers. The leader of Dhuma offered a large amount of booty and agreed to pay protection tax. The chiefs of Eilah, Herbah, and Azrah also followed him. The Prophet (ﷺ) had written a truce for them, The Prophet (ﷺ) returned to Madinah and managed the Muslims who could not join him. Three true Muslims were reprimanded for fifty days because the Prophet (ﷺ) stayed out on their expedition for fifty days. Therefore, their social boycott was for the same period.

The battle created positive effects on the other tribes. Most of them embraced Islam within a brief period of two years prior to the death of the Prophet (ﷺ). The people of Arab started to support Muslims who were under the influence of Romans. It helped Muslim to concentrate on learning and teaching and expanding the message of Islam to the remaining areas of the Arab lands.

The information Startegy

Information management is important for any organisation because managers can make informed decisions based upon right and timely input. Tabuk was a military project which depends on the timing and quality of

---

[34] P. 318.

information. The awareness of enemy intentions, preparation and strength are vital for formulation of effective strategy. This chapter is reserved to know the information strategy of the Prophet (ﷺ).

Information management

Association of Project Management (APM) defines information management (IM) as "information management is the collection, storage, dissemination, archiving and destruction of information. It enables teams and stakeholders to use their time, resource and expertise effectively to make decisions and to fulfil their roles."[35] It involves gathering and conveying of accurate information on time.

Gathering information

The Prophet (ﷺ) had developed a network of gathering and communicating information in connection with the expedition. The network of the Prophet (ﷺ) was formal as well as informal. The formal network was based upon its own people while the informal systems depended upon the traders and other people. For example, the traders of oil informed that Hercules had collected an army of 40,000 people including the Arab troops. The army was under the leadership of a great commander of Room. They had sent an advanced party to Belqa. Consequently, the Prophet (ﷺ) had ordered the army to assemble in Madinah including confederate Arabs and people from Makkah.

---

[35] https://www.apm.org.uk/body-of-knowledge/delivery/integrative-management/information-management/

The written record was kept entering the names of all the participants. Similarly, all the donations were also recorded as we have described in one of the tables in the earlier chapters. The purpose was to keep the record of all people and the donations. In addition, information was also kept in mind (tacit knowledge) about those who did not participate including the true Muslims about which we have discussed in the previous chapters. An informal record of hypocrites was also kept. It was the basis of actions taken against non-participants and the hypocrites. When limited resources were given to the substantial number of troops, calculation was made about how many people can ride an animal. It has been reported that eighteen people were sharing one camel.

Written communication

The Prophet (ﷺ) also use treaties in black and White with many heads of States including the people of Eelah, Jerbah, and Azruh. The text of the truce was,

"In the Name of Allâh, the Most Beneficent, the Most Merciful.

This is a guarantee of protection from Allâh and Muhammad the Prophet (ﷺ), the Messenger of Allâh, to Yahna bin Rawbah and the people of Ailah; their ships, their caravans on land and sea shall have the custody of Allâh and the Prophet (ﷺ) Muhammad, he and whosoever are with him of Ash-Sham people and those of the sea. Whosoever contravenes this treaty, his wealth shall not save him; it shall be his fair prize that takes it. Now it should not be lawful to hinder the men from any springs which they have been in the habit of frequenting, nor from any journeys they wish to make, whether by sea or by land."[36]

Statistics was also kept about the number of people. The counts were maintained for the total number of participants,[37] the small expedition sent under the command of Khalid Bin Waleed (RA) to the leader of Dhumatul Jandal, the number of troops with him was 420.[38] There were 4 true Muslims who could not participate.[39] The duration of the campaign was 50 days, the Islamic army stayed in Tabuk for 20 days. The number of hypocrites left behind was more than eighty.[40]

In connection with one of the peace pacts, the Prophet (ﷺ) had done with the leader of Dhomatul Jundhal. The account was kept for the booty they had collected from him. It includes two thousand Camels, eight hundred slave, four hundred shields and four hundred spears.

In addition, on the way back twelve hypocrites try to harm the Prophet (ﷺ). The cleaver eyes of the Prophet (ﷺ) were upon them, and he knew their intentions, as a result, he sent Huzaifa Razi Allah Tala anhu to counter them. Allah (SWT) had created fear in their minds and they could not dare to achieve their goals. Note that the Prophet had not taken revenge despite the mischiefs of the opponents.

---

[36] Mubarikpuri, p. 586-87.

[37] Shibli, total 30,000 including 10,000 horse riders, p. 336.

[38] Phalwarvi says they were 400 (p. 507).

[39] Lings, p. 319.

[40] Siddiqui, p. 506; Phalwarvi says they were approximately 82. (p. 506)

Dissemination of information

One purpose of information system is to give information to subordinates including managers so that they can make informed decisions. The Prophet (ﷺ) had informed the subordinates where to go before starting the journey. He had sent people to inform the forces of Arabs and people of Mecca to join him for the expedition. On the way to the Tabuk, Muslim army had to travel through the area of Saleh (AS). The Prophet (ﷺ) informed them that they travel fast from the area, but you can drink water from the well from where the she-camel of Saleh (AS) used to drink. When he reached the destination, he informed the companions that there would be a storm so be careful about it.

The Prophet (ﷺ) regularly informed those companions who could not participate in the expedition about the decision of Almighty. For instance, for up to 40 days there was social boycott with these people and afterwards, more severe decision was made. They were informed that they should also get separate from their wives. At the end, the good news was communicated to them that their punishments had finished, and their repentance had been accepted. It was announced openly through another companion. Therefore, everybody listened to the announcement. There was a smile on the faces of everyone on this occasion. It suggests that he has kept the flow of information systematically and in an efficient manner. It could be one of the reasons for the success of the expedition.

When the Prophet (ﷺ) reached the destination, he delivered a comprehensive lecture to motivate people for the expedition telling them the virtues of fighting in the cause of Allah (SWT) and the rewards Allah (SWT) has kept for those who strive in the path of Allah (SWT). He also described the punishment of Allah (SWT) for those who hesitate to spend their time and money in the path of Allah (SWT).

In nutshell

We understand that the Prophet (ﷺ) are sent to convey the message of Allah (SWT) to their nations. They receive the information from Him and give them to the masses. People used to memories and write Devine revelation. The companions had done the same; it helped Usman (RA) to compile the words of Almighty in the form of a book later. The second chapter of the holy book states in the beginning that this book is free of doubt.

The Prophet (ﷺ) had applied the same strategy to manage the expedition. In addition to other aspects, we can say that the Prophet (ﷺ) had managed information effectively and efficiently. The key points of his strategy were:

- Constantly kept informed the stakeholders.
- Applied formal and informal sources.
- Allah (SWT) used to inform him of hidden aspects such as the intentions of hypocrites.
- The written record was kept systematically.
- Humans were the primary source of collection and dissemination of information. The tacit knowledge was in the memories of people. It could be extracted/retrieved as and when needed.

5 CASE STUDY: THE TREATY OF HODHABIA

The brief account of the event

There are several reasons for the choice of Hodhabia as a case study. First, it was the non-fighting expedition of the Prophet (ﷺ). Secondly, he had avoided a war due to his vigilance and foresight. Thirdly, he had negotiated with Quraysh while previous encounters were armed 'meetings. The Prophet (ﷺ) had to manage his companions because of the conditions of the treaty which were defensive in nature. And the Prophet (ﷺ) was given glad tiding of 'disguised glory' in the apparent retreat. The Divine Will was with the Prophet (ﷺ). "The Hudaibiyah encounter occurred meanwhile that not only gave Muslims courage to go ahead with the mission, but it also tested their courage and faith in Islam."[41]

The drivers of the campaign

---

[41] Hijazi, Abu Tariq (2012) Hudaibiyah: A turning point in the history of Islam, http://www.arabnews.com/hudaibiyah-turning-point-history-islam

According to Lings[42] one night towards its end he dreamed that with his head shaved he entered the Ka'bah, and its key was in his hand. The next day he told his Companions of this and invited them to perform the Lesser Pilgrimage with him, whereupon they hastily set about preparing so that they could leave as soon as possible. Between them, they purchased seventy camels to be sacrificed in the sacred precinct. Their meat would then be distributed among the poor of Mecca. The Prophet (ﷺ) decided to take one of his wives with him, and when lots were cast the lot fell to Umm Salamah (RA).

Consequently, he has announced in and around Madinah about his intention of performing Umrah. He appointed two companions as his deputy and marched towards Makkah in 6 A.H. with 1400 companions. He wore ihram and prepared animals for sacrifice at Zulhalifah (The boundary of harum from Madinah side).

He had also appointed an intelligence officer to know the possible reaction of Quraysh or other tribes. The officer informed him at Asfaan and described the plans of enemy tribes during the journey. They were getting prepared to stop the Prophet (ﷺ) on the way to his destination.

The Prophet (ﷺ) consulted his team and put forward two proposals: to fight with these tribes and clear the way to reach Makkah, or avoid them and continue the journey. He opted the later scheme. Meanwhile, the Prophet (ﷺ) came to know that Quraysh was also in fighting 'mode' and they had dispatched a squad of 200 horse riders under the command of Khalid bin Waleed through another intelligence source. Khalid was planning to attack while

---

[42] P. 247

Muslims were supposed to pray salat. Allah (SWT) sent down the special order of praying in the battlefield. It restricted the enemy to take advantage of the opportunity. On top of that, the Prophet (ﷺ) changed his way to avoid any encounter with Quraysh. The path was difficult and rocky, but he continued till Hodhabia and encamped there near a small water well.

The negotiation

Tribes of Khaza was a confederate of Muslims, some of them approached the Prophet (ﷺ) and explained him the plans of Quraysh. Badheel bin Warqa informed him that they would never allow you to enter Makkah. The Prophet (ﷺ) said they were not there to fight but if they would be forced to do so "I swear to Allah (SWT) that I will fight with them for the cause of my mission until I get martyred or they would be defeated".[43] Nevertheless, he put a peace proposal for them. Badheel conveyed the message to Quraysh who sent their ambassador for further conversation.

Both sides exchanged their views through representatives but without outcome because Quraysh was die-heart. They sent a group of 70/80 warriors secretly to attack Muslims to damage the peace talks. Muslims guards captured them, but the Prophet (ﷺ) released them as a positive gesture to continue peace efforts.

The Prophet (ﷺ) had deputed Usman (RA) to talk to Quraysh after consultation with others. He was selected because he was a respectable person of mild temperament,

---

[43] Mobarikpuri, p. 462.

and his clan was still in Makkah. In case of an accident, his clan could help him out. The Prophet (ﷺ) advised him:
- Tell them that we are peaceful.
- Invite them to Islam
- Give glad tiding to the Muslim still living in Makkah about the dominance of Islam in Makkah soon.

Usman (RA) conveyed the message of the Prophet (ﷺ) to the key figures of Quraysh. They offered him to do tawaf of Kaaba, but he refused. Quraysh asked him to stay a little bit more so that they could decide about the outcome of the conversation.

Meanwhile, a rumour reached the Prophet (ﷺ) that Usman (RA) was got martyred. The Prophet (ﷺ) reacted quickly and asked his companions to get prepare for a battle. He took famous pledge known in the Islamic history as "Bait-e-Rizwaan". It was the pledge of the fight for the cause of Allah (SWT) and to remain steadfast in the battlefield. However, soon after it, Usman (RA) returned, and he took the same as well.

Quraysh got the message and immediately sent their mediator. The competing parties arrived at a truce at last. Some conditions were against the Muslims but other conditions provided them strength. Quraysh was forced to accept Islam as a force/party which compelled them to allow Muslims to do Umrah the following year.

The glad tidings of victory

Allah (SWT) gave glad tidings of victory to the Prophet (ﷺ). Muslims officially included their confederate (i.e. Banu Khaza) in their ranks. Doors opened to other tribes to join hands with Muslims. The treaty offered a decade of peace for them. Peace always supports Muslim cause because it provides an opportunity for Muslims to present their message to others. War used to be a source of bloodshed that increases the gulf of hatred. It creates a communication gap that hinders non-Muslims to study and understand Islam.

Muslims were under moral pressure when Abu Jandal (RA) arrived and solicit the help of the Prophet(ﷺ). The Prophet (ﷺ) tried to settle down his matter, but the negotiator was his father who was not ready at any cost to leave him with Muslims. The Prophet (ﷺ) advised him, "be patient". He said to the nearest effect that Allah (SWT) would open a door of salvation for you and all those who were suffering from the hands of infidels.

The inforamtion strategy

There are several reasons for the selection of Hodhabia as a case study. First, it was the non-fighting expedition of the Prophet (ﷺ). Secondly, he had avoided a war due to his vigilance and foresight. Thirdly, he had negotiated with Quraysh while previous encounters were armed 'meetings. The Prophet (ﷺ) had to manage his companions because of the conditions of the treaty which were defensive in nature. And the Prophet (ﷺ) was given glad tiding of 'disguised glory' in the apparent retreat. The Divine Will was with the Prophet (ﷺ). "The Hudaibiyah encounter occurred meanwhile that not only gave Muslims courage to go ahead with the mission, but it also tested their courage and faith in Islam."[44]

Managing information

---

[44] Hijazi, Abu Tariq (2012) Hudaibiyah: A turning point in the history of Islam, http://www.arabnews.com/hudaibiyah-turning-point-history-islam

First, he disseminated information about his intention or programme to the inhabitants of Madinah and the other Muslims of the time. It implies that managers should inform everyone for any initiative the organisation wanted to take in the future. He had applied the available channels of communication; the human medium was one of the powerful tools, so the Prophet (ﷺ) had used it.

The Prophet (ﷺ) had appointed one of his colleagues to function as a deputy to his job. He used to lead prayers and managing the day-to-day affairs of the city, in fact, the newly born state of Madinah. All managers should appoint a second-hand command whenever they are out of the station.

It is important to know the movements of opponents in the war or in marketing/business management. Management information systems is a current way to gather information. The Prophet (ﷺ) had appointed an information officer to keep an eye on the activities of enemies. He received the news that some tribes on the way to Makkah were getting prepared for an armed encounter. Since the purpose of the journey did not coincide with the situation on ground, therefore, he avoided them. The Prophet (ﷺ) also kept himself away from the possible interference of Quraysh's military squad. It suggests that he *focused* on his objective. Contemporary management writers believe it as a key function of a Chief Executive Officer (CEO).[45] Nevertheless, when Badheel informed him about the intentions of Quraysh, he reiterated his intention and had shown his determination to implement/achieve his mission at any cost. His determination forced Quraysh to rethink about their plan to stop

---

[45] Johnson, Rick (2018) The Four Primary Functions of CEO Leadership, Retrieved from http://www.groco.com/readingroom/bus_ceoleadership_functions.aspx.

him at all costs. Consequently, they sent their envoy to commence a dialogue. It suggests the Prophet (ﷺ) was guiding his followers consistently. [46]

The Prophet (ﷺ) had deputed Usman (RA) for further talks. He went to Makkah and did his job. Meanwhile, a rumour circulated about the martyrdom of Usman (RA). The Prophet(ﷺ) reacted immediately and took an oath from his companions for a war. It forced Quraysh to start a negotiation. The new envoy completed the peace talks which ended at a truce. Thus, the Prophet (ﷺ) had achieved his objective out of the journey.

He encountered a challenge from the companions when they did not respond about his decision to abandon Umrah and return to Madinah as per the conditions of the treaty. He resolved it amicably as well. He started to conclude the Umrah by shaving his head and changing the special dress. The companions followed him. Thus, he presented himself as what is called in management literature as "Role model".[47] We can summarise his decisions and actions as shown in table 2.

Table 2 Summary of the Prophet's (ﷺ) decisions		
Triggers	**Decision**	**Impact**
Dream/Devine order	Do Umrah	Truce of Hodhabia
His movement towards Makkah	Avoid enemies	Enemies failed to stop him

---

[46] Experts believe a CEO "guides courses of action in operations", from "Roles and Responsibilities of Chief Executive Officer of a corporation", Retrieved from https://managementhelp.org/chiefexecutives/job-description.htm#roles.

[47] Smith, p. 364.

Allah's (SWT) command (Need for a peace truce)	Initiated talks	Achieved peace and long-term victory
Enemy attack but Muslim army captured the invaders	Set them freed	Created positive image about Muslims
Non-compliance of companions for abandoning Umrah	He started the initiative	The issue was resolved

6 CASE STUDY: THE HIJRAH EXPEDITION

The story the expedition
Since the migration was the most illustrious incident in the history of Islam and in fact in the history of the world because the incident transformed the fate of people forever, therefore, it seems appropriate to describe it in this context. The Prophet went to Taaif for expanding his reach of the work of dawah; he also sent two delegations to Abyssinia, but no meaningful results came out. He was in search of a place where he can transfer his "headquarter" to set up a base of dawah. He used to invite pilgrims of that time in the hajj season. But until eleventh years no one accepted his message. Six persons from Madinah took the lead in this year and accepted Islam. The next year they became twelve and the following year seventy-two. Now Yathrib was ready to welcome the Prophet (ﷺ) and his followers. The chapter is describing the event.

Background
When the Prophet (ﷺ) received the first revelation, his wife took him to one of the monks of the time, Warqa bin Nofil. Mobarikpuri (1995) writes,
"She set out with the Prophet (ﷺ) to her cousin Waraqa bin Nawfal bin Asad bin 'Abd Al- 'Uzza, who had embraced

Christianity in the pre-Islamic period, and used to write the Bible in Hebrew. He was a blind old man. Khadijah said: "My cousin! Listen to your nephew!" Waraqa said: "O my nephew! What did you see?" The Messenger of Allâh told him what had happened to him. Waraqa replied: "This is *'Namus'* i.e. (the angel who is entrusted with Divine Secrets) that Allâh sent to Moses. I wish I were younger. I wish I could live up to the time when your people would turn you out." Muhammad (asked: "Will they drive me out?" Waraqa answered in the affirmative and said: "Anyone who came with something similar to what you have brought was treated with hostility; and if I should be alive till that day, then I would support you strongly." [48]

It implies that Hijrah was destined. The Prophet (ﷺ) had to leave his cherished home and hometown. He sent two groups of his companions to Abyssinia in search of a proper place for the future base camp of Islam but could not receive the positive response. He also travelled to Taif for the same purpose, but the journey was fruitless. However, there was hope of betterment in the new destination.

Quraysh had created difficult circumstances for the Prophet (ﷺ) and his followers to remain in Makkah. The Prophet (ﷺ) was in search of an alternative place to continue his mission. He started planning for it when he invited the delegates of Madinah towards Islam during the Hajj period. Fortunately, some of them embraced his message. A larger group took shelter under the shade of Islam later. When they came to know that Muslims were in hardship in Makkah, they invited them to Madinah to avoid the difficulties they were facing. Consequently, the famous

---

[48] P. 99.

treaty of Mina took place. Muslims started to leave Makkah individually or in small groups to avoid an open battle with the infidels.

Quraysh came to know about the plan of the Prophet (ﷺ) to leave Makkah and settled down in Madinah, a safe place for him and his companions. They conspired for the assignation of the Prophet (ﷺ). Molana Kandhelvi described it.

"Hadhrat Urwa narrates that after the Hajj season, Rasulullaah (ﷺ) was in Makkah during the remaining days of Dhulijjah, Muharram and Safar. The Mushrikeen then gathered to conspire against him, thinking that he would soon be leaving Makkah since they knew that Allaah had created a place of safety and protection for him in Madinah. They had also found out that the Ansaar had accepted Islaam and that the Muhaajireen were going to them. The Mushrikeen, therefore, planned to capture Rasulullaah (ﷺ) and then either assassinate him, imprison him., exile him or keep him tied up. Allaah informed Rasulullaah (ﷺ) about their plot and revealed the following verse:

(o Muhammad (ﷺ) Remember the time) When the Kuffaar schemed against you to imprison you, kill you or exile you (drive you out of Makkah). They plan and Allaah plans. Allaah is the best of planners." (Surah Anfaal: 30)

The day when Rasulullaah (ﷺ) went to the house of Hadhrat Abu Bakr (رضي الله عنه), Nabi (ﷺ) was informed that the Mushrikeen planned to assassinate him as he slept that night."[49]

Quraysh wanted to kill him because it was the viable way for them. Previous Prophets (AS) were also murdered by

---

[49] Kaandhlawi (2012), v. p.339.

their nations. The ignorant people do not have any logical or ethical argument in the history of mankind against Prophets (AS). Force is and was the only alternative, so, Quraysh were thinking in the same way because they were illiterate and inconsiderate. The Prophet (ﷺ) responded because it was the right time for him to start the sacred journey.

Preparation

Allah (SWT) had decided the timing and Abu Bakr (رضي الله عنه) arranged the resources. Hadhrat Aiysha (رضي الله عنه) says, "Rasulullaah (ﷺ) said, 'Allaah has permitted me to migrate and to leave Makkah. Hadhrat Abu Bakr (رضي الله عنه), asked May I accompany you? Rasulullah replied, "Certainly," replied Rasulullaah (ﷺ). Hadhrat Abu Bakr (رضي الله عنه) said, "I have two camels that I have been rearing from a long time in anticipation for this day. You may take one." Rasulullaah (ﷺ) said, "Only at a price, Abu Bakr." Hadhrat Abu Bakr (رضي الله عنه) replied, "May my parents be sacrificed for you". You may have it at a price if you, so wish." [50]Thus, the required resources were available. The plan of the infidels to eliminate the source of guidance was about to fail. Allah (SWT) had a plan to eliminate *kuffer* from the sacred land forever. And it had happened after only a few years. Many of the prominent companions like Umer (رضي الله عنه) and Hamza (رضي الله عنه) already left. Ali (رضي الله عنه) and Abu Bakr (رضي الله عنه) were still in the native town. Abu Bakr (رضي الله عنه) wanted to emigrate, but the Prophet (ﷺ) asked him to wait.

---

[50] Kaandhlawi (2012), p.341.

Quraysh did everything to stop Muslims but failed. Lings states some details about the situation interestingly. He says,

"Quraysh did what they could to stop the emigrations. Suhayl's other daughter had now gone with her husband Abu Hudhayfah, just as they had previously gone to Abyssinia, but Suhayl was determined that this time his son Abd Allah should not escape him, so he kept a close watch on him. Much the same happened to the son of the Sahmite leader 'As, Hisham, who likewise had been among the emigrants to Abyssinia. It was his half-brother 'Amr who had been sent by Quraysh to turn the Negus against the Muslim refugees, and Hisham had witnessed his failure and discomforting. 'Urnar, who was Hisham's cousin - their mothers were sisters - had arranged that they should now travel to Yathrib together, leaving Mecca separately and meeting at the thorn-trees of Adat about ten miles north of the city. 'Ayyash of Makhzum was also to travel with them; but at the appointed hour and place there was no sign of Hisham, so 'Umar and his family went on their way with 'Ayyash, for they had agreed that they would not wait for each other. Hisham's father and brother had heard of his plan and held him back by force, and they put so much pressure on him that after some days they even persuaded him to renounce Islam."[51]

The companions were on the way to Yathrib despite all odds. And the Prophet (ﷺ) must join them.

---

[51] Lings, p. 114.

The journey

The Prophet (ﷺ) left when most of the companions reached Madinah. The journey itself was an example of a well-planned venture. Molana Yusaf Kandhelvi writes,

"Under the veil of the night, Rasulullaah (ﷺ) and Hadhrat Abu Bakr (رضي الله عنه) left for the cave in the Thowr mountain, which is mentioned in the holy Qur'an. Hadhrat Ali bin Abi Taalib (رضي الله عنه) slept on Rasulullah's (ﷺ) bed so that Rasulullaah (ﷺ) could hide from Mushrikeen spies (who would think that Rasulullaah (ﷺ) is asleep in the house). The Mushrikeen spend the night walking about and discussing how they would leap on to the person sleeping and tie him up. They continued in this manner until dawn broke and they saw Hadhrat Ali (رضي الله عنه) stand up from Rasulullah's (ﷺ) bed. When they asked Hadhrat Ali (رضي الله عنه) where Rasulullaah (ﷺ) was, he said that he did not know."[52]

The reaction: They then realised that Rasulullaah (ﷺ) had left Makkah. Molana continue the topic, he says,

"The Mushrikeen then took to their mounts and started searching for Rasulullah. (ﷺ). They also sent messages to the people at the various oases, instructing them to capture Rasulullaah (ﷺ) and promising them large rewards. They reached the cave of Thowr; here Rasulullaah (ﷺ) and Hadhrat Abu Bakr (رضي الله عنه) hid and had even climbed on top of the cave (where the entrance was). Rasulullaah (ﷺ) heard their voices and Hadhrat Abu Bakr (رضي الله عنه) became worried and frightened. Rasulullaah (ﷺ) then said to him.

---

[52] V.1 p. 340.

"... Do not grieve (do not fear for my safety). Verily Allaah is with us (and He will protect us from the Kuffaar) ... " {Surah Taubah: 40)

Rasulullaah (ﷺ) then made du'aa to Allaah and Allaah sent peace and tranquillity to them as referred to in the following verse:

. . . So Allaah (SWT) caused His tranquillity (serenity, mercy, and peace) to descend on him, assisted him with an army (of angels and other creation) that you had not seen. And (Allaah (SWT)) placed the word of the Kuffaar (the call to Shirk) at the very bottom while the word of Allaah (the Kalimah) is right at the top. Allaah is Mighty, The Wise. {Surah Taubah: 40).53

The enemy was searching continuously, in the words of Maulana Yusaf Kandhelvi, "When they arrived at the cave, Hadhrat Abu Bakr (رضي الله عنه) entered first and placed his finger in every hole, fearing that there may be an insect there (which would harm Rasulullaah (ﷺ). When the Quraysh found out that they were gone, they set out in search of them and fixed a reward of a hundred camels for anyone who captured Rasulullaah (ﷺ). They scoured the mountains of Makkah and eventually reached the mountain where Rasulullaah (ﷺ) and Hadhrat Abu Bakr (رضي الله عنه) were hiding. Referring to a person who was facing the cave, Hadhrat Abu Bakr (رضي الله عنه) said, "o Rasulullaah (ﷺ) they will surely see us." "Never," replied Rasulullaah (ﷺ), *"because the angels are hiding us with their wings."* Still facing the cave, the man then sat down to pass urine. Rasulullaah (ﷺ) said, "Had he seen us,

---

53 V. 1, p. 340.

he would never have done that." [54] The noble team stayed there for three days.

Kandhlavi writes further about the journey. "Hadhrat Abu Bakr (رضي الله عنه) had several milk-giving goats that would be brought to him and taken to his family in Makkah. He also had an honest and trustworthy slave by the name of Hadhrat Aamir bin Fuhayra (رضي الله عنه) who was an incredibly good Muslim. Hadhrat Abu Bakr (رضي الله عنه) sent him to hire a guide (to take them to Madinah) and Hadhrat Aamir (رضي الله عنه) hired a man called Ibnul Ayqadh. He belonged to the Banu Abd bin Adi tribe who were allies of the Banu Sahm branch of the Banu Aas bin Waa'il tribe that belonged to the Quraysh. This guide from the Banu Adi tribe was a Mushrik then and it was his occupation to guide people on the journeys. During those nights (that they hid the cave), the two of them (Hadhrat Aamir (رضي الله عنه) and the guide) hid in the camels of Rasulullaah (ﷺ) and Hadhrat Abu Bakr (رضي الله عنه) while Hadhrat Abdullah (رضي الله عنه) the son of Hadhrat Abu Bakr (رضي الله عنه) would come to them every evening and relate to them the events taking place in Makkah. Every night, Hadhrat Aamir (رضي الله عنه) would bring them some goats, which they would milk and then slaughter one to eat. Early in the mornings, he would take the goats away to the grazing fields that the people used for their goats and no one realised what was happening."[55]

---

[54] Kandhlavi (2012), p.339-344.

[55] Kandhlavi (2012), p. 340-341.

Towards Madinah

"This continued until talk of Rasulullaah (ﷺ) and Hadhrat Abu Bakr (رضي الله عنه) died down and they learnt that things were quiet. Their two companions then arrived with the camels, and they left. They had already been in the cave for two days and two nights. They took Hadhrat Aamir bin Fuhayra (رضي الله عنه) along with them, who drove the camels, served them, and assisted them. Hadhrat Abu Bakr (رضي الله عنه) would let him ride the camel behind him in turns. Besides Hadhrat Aamir (رضي الله عنه) and the guide from the Banu Adi, no one else accompanied Rasulullaah (ﷺ) and Hadhrat Abu Bakr (رضي الله عنه).

(After three nights) Rasulullaah (ﷺ) and Hadhrat Abu Bakr (رضي الله عنه) left the cave and took a route along the coast. Hadhrat Abu Bakr (رضي الله عنه) travelled in front of Rasulullaah (ﷺ) but whenever he felt any danger from the rear, he travelled at the back. The entire journey passed in this manner. Hadhrat Abu Bakr (رضي الله عنه) was a well-known man. Therefore, whenever someone met him, they asked who was with him. He would reply, "He is a guide who is showing me the way." By saying this, he meant that Rasulullaah (ﷺ) was guiding him in Deen, but the person thought that Rasulullaah (ﷺ) was someone showing him the road. When they reached the settlement of Qudayd which lay on their route, someone told the Banu Mudlaj tribe (who lived there), "I have seen two riders near the coast. I think that they are the men from the Quraysh whom you are searching for." Suraaqa bin Maalik said to the person, "Those are two men whom we have sent out to do some work for the people." (Suraaqa knew that that the riders were Rasulullaah (ﷺ) and Hadhrat Abu Bakr (رضي الله عنه) said this so that he could have them to himself and earn the reward). Suraaqa then called for his slave woman and whispered to her to get his horse. He then set out on the trail of Rasulullaah (ﷺ) and Hadhrat Abu Bakr (رضي الله عنه).

Hadhrat Abu Bakr (رضي الله عنه) related, "We left (the cave) early at night and travelled speedily the entire day and night the afternoon when the heat became intense. I then strained my eye to see whether I could see any shade to take shelter. When I spotted a large boulder, I hurried to it and found that it still offered some shade. I then levelled the ground for Rasulullaah (ﷺ) and spread out a coat for him. I then bade him lie down and he did. Thereafter, I went to see whether I could spot anyone who was searching for us." Hadhrat Abu Bakr (رضي الله عنه) related further, "When I saw a shepherd and asked him who he worked for, he took the name of a man from the Quraysh whom I knew. 'Do any of the goats have milk?' I asked. Yes,' he replied. 'Will you milk some for me?' I enquired. When he agreed, he held the animal still as I had asked. I then asked him to wipe off the sand from the udders (which he did with his hands), and I then asked him to dust his hands off. I had a container with me that had a cloth tied to the mouth. After he had milked a bit of milk for me, I threw water onto a cup so that its bottom got cold (and the milk as well). I then went to Rasulullaah (ﷺ) and found him awake. I said, 'Drink, o Rasulullaah (ﷺ). He then drank so much that I became pleased. 'Is it not time to leave?' I spoke. We then left." "Although people were searching for us, no one caught up with us besides Suraaqa bin Maalik bin Ju'shum, who did so on his horse. (Seeing him approach), I said, "o Rasulullaah (ﷺ) here comes someone in search of us. He has caught up with us.' Rasulullaah (ﷺ) said, 'Do not grieve because Allah (SWT) is with us.' When Suraaqa drew close and was only the distance of one or two spear-lengths away from us, I cried and said, 'o Rasulullaah (ﷺ), he has caught up with us!' Rasulullaah (ﷺ) said, 'What makes you weep?' I replied, 'I swear by Allah (SWT) that it is not for my own safety that I weep but I am crying for your safety.' Rasulullaah (ﷺ) then made du'aa saying, 'o Allah (SWT)! Deal with him on our behalf as You please.' Suraaqa's horse suddenly sank into the ground up to its belly although the ground was hard. Suraaqa sprang off the horse and said, 'o Muhammad! I know that you have done this. Please pray to Allah (SWT) to save me from this predicament and I swear by Allah (SWT) that I shall throw every other tracker I meet off your trail. Take an arrow from my quiver here and when you pass by a certain place where you will see my camels and goats (show this arrow to the shepherds) and take whatever you need.' Rasulullaah (ﷺ) said, 'I have no need for that.' Rasulullaah (ﷺ) then made du'aa to Allah (SWT) and Suraaqa was freed. He then returned to his people." "Rasulullah (ﷺ) and I continued until we reached Madinah where the people came to welcome him. They climbed the roofs on either side of the road as servants and children ran on the road saying, 'Allah (SWT) u Akbar! Rasulullaah (ﷺ) had arrived! Muhammad (ﷺ) has come!' When the people started quarrelling about who would be his host, Rasulullaah (ﷺ) said, 'I shall stay the night with the Banu Najjaar tribe who are the maternal relatives of Abdul Muttalib so that I may honour them.' The following morning, Rasulullaah (ﷺ) stayed where he was commanded to stay (by Allah (SWT))."[56]

---

[56] Kandhelvi (2012), p. 345-346.

Information management (IM)

Association of Project Management defines it as, "Information management is the collection, storage, dissemination, archiving, and destruction of information. It enables teams and stakeholders to use their time, resource, and expertise effectively to make decisions and to fulfil their roles."57 The Business Dictionary states that it is the "Application of management techniques to *collect* information, *communicate* it within and outside the organization, and *process* it to enable managers to make quicker and better decisions."58 The second one is more relevant in the scenario. Three italic words in the definition need explanation.

Collection

The first task was to *collect* information. The Prophet (ﷺ) had appointed Ali (رضي الله عنه) to return the items kept with him for safe keeping. The Prophet (ﷺ) felt the obligation to return the property of those who trusted him as "trustworthy". The Prophet (ﷺ) wanted to receive information for safe disposal of the property to their owners.

Second Abdullah bin Abu Bakr (رضي الله عنه) was appointed as information officer to collect information about the

---

57 https://www.apm.org.uk/body-of-knowledge/delivery/integrative-management/information-management/

58 http://www.businessdictionary.com/definition/information-management.html

activities of Quraysh. He used to stay in Makkah during daytime and collect relevant information. And used to *communicate* it to the noble team in the evening. It enabled the Prophet (ﷺ) to keep an eye on the activities of his opponents i.e. to make informed decisions.

The contemporary business owns or have access to a lot of information; they select and *process* them. The information officer of the Prophet (ﷺ) listened to a bundle of information, but he communicated only the relevant piece of it to the noble team. In this way, he processed (including filtering it) information to convey the required one.

Secrecy of information

Keeping some information secret is an important act of information management. These days organisation make them "classified" so that certain people can access them because they are their business secrets. It gives them competitive advantage.[59] During the expedition of Hijrah the Prophet (ﷺ) wanted to hide the whereabouts of his team. Consequently, the shepherd was running over the footprints of the team in the first instance when he travelled to the cave. Thereafter, the same person was doing same action for Abdullah bin Abu Bakr (رضي الله عنه) who was travelling to and from Makkah for three days. It kept Quraysh unaware about the Prophet (ﷺ) and his colleague.

---

[59] Porter, M E and Victor E. Millar (1985) How Information Gives You Competitive Advantage, Harvard Business Review, July issue.

The Prophet (ﷺ) had signed migration treaty with the Muslims of Madinah secretly. Quraysh were unaware about it when it took its existence. Most of the Muslims took their way to Madinah silently except Umer (RA). The Prophet (ﷺ) did not show his intention of migration until last minutes. He shared it with Abu Bakr (RA) because he was his companion in the journey. When Saraaqa approached the noble team and his horse sunk in the ground. He begged for the release of his horse. The Prophet (ﷺ) made dua for him. Saraaqa offered some things to him, but he said, "keep the whereabouts of our secret".[60]

These examples show the strategy of the Prophet (ﷺ) to keep secrecy because it was and is a tool for information management. Countries and organisation keep their information secret as their "business secret" to gain competitive advantage.

Dissemination

The Prophet (ﷺ) informed his companions about the pact of Mina and silently allowed them to begin movement towards Madinah. Similarly, he went himself to Abu Bakr (RA) to inform him about the Devine permission for migration. Therefore, the distribution of information at right time and in right amount made the journey success.

It implies that the Prophet (ﷺ) obtained the required information and kept the opponents away from what information they needed. It was one of the reasons that the noble team arrived in Madinah unharmed because it happened due to the effective management of information.

---

[60] Mubarikpuri, p. 237.

If we look at the successful organisations/countries today, they do the same to get a competitive advantage in their area of interest. One of the experts in management argues that information gives organisations a competitive advantage.[61] The Hijrah completed with the effective management of information.

---

[61] Porter, M E and Victor E. Millar (1985) How Information Gives You Competitive Advantage, Harvard Business Review, July issue.

BIBLIOGRAPHY

Adair, John (2010) The Leadership of Muhammad (PBUH), New Delhi: Kogan Page India Private Limited.

Al-Bahaqi, Abi Bakker Ahmad Al-Hussain (2009) Dhalail Al-Nabuwwa, Karachi: Dharul Ishaat.

Alnoor Holdings Group (2011) The Prophet of Islam MUHAMMAD, Biography & Practical Guide to the Moral Bases of the Islamic Civilization, Alnoor Holdings Group Qatar.

Allen, Louis A. (1958) Management and organization, New York: McGraw-Hill.

Chesbrough, H. W. "The era of open innovation." MIT Sloan Management Review 44, no. 3 (2003a): 35-41.

Chesbrough, H. W. Open Innovation: The New Imperative for Creating and Profiting from Technology. (Boston: Harvard Business Press, 2003b)

Chesbrough, H. W. 2006. "The era of open innovation." In Managing Innovation and Change, edited by David Moyle, 127-138. London: Sage Publications Ltd.

DeCenzo, David A. and Stephen P. Robbins (2010) Human Resource Management, New York: John Wiley & Sons.

Dess, Gregory G., G. T. Lumpkin, Alan B. Eisner (2006) Strategic Management: Text and Cases, New York: Irwin/McGraw-Hill.

Dyck, B and Mitchell J Neubert (2009) Principal of Management, South-Western.

Fulop, L, and S Linstead (1999) Management, A critical text, London: Macmillan.

Gilani, Mnazar Ahsan Gilani (1936) Al-Nabi Al-Khatam Sallallaho Alaihay Wasallam (Urdu), Jayyad Barqi Press: Dehli.

Haimann, Theo and Raymond L. Hilgert (1972) Supervision: Concepts and Practices of Management, South-Western Publishing Company.

Hameed Ullah, M. (2006) The Prophet's (ﷺ) Establishing a State and his Succession, Beacon Books: Lahore.

Haykal, Muhammad Husayn, Translated by Isma'il Razi A. al-Faruqi, The Life of Muhammad (ﷺ)http://www.witness-pioneer.org/vil/Books/MH_LM/default.htm

Ibn Ishaq Sirat Rasoul Allah, An abridged version, https://ia800206.us.archive.org/12/items/Sirat-lifeOfMuhammad By-ibnIshaq/SiratIbnIahaqInEnglish.pdf

Iqbal, Javed, and Muhammad Mushtaq Ahmad (2009) Planning in the Islamic Tradition: The Case of Hijrah Expedition, INSIGHTS 01(3), 37-68.

Kaandhlawi, Muhammad Zakarya (1997), Fazail-e-Amaal, Lahore: Kutibkhana Faizi.

Kaandhlawi, Muhammad Yusaf (2012), Hayatus Sahabah, Delhi: Islamic Books Services.

Koontz, Harold, and Heinz Weihrich (2006) Essentials of Management, New Delhi: Tata McGraw-Hill Education, pp. 81-84.

Kreitner, R (2009) Principal of Management, South-Western.

Lings, M (1994) Muhammad, his life based on the earliest sources, Lahore: Suhail Academy.

Mayo, E. (1933), The Human Problems of an Industrial Organization, McMillan, New York, NY.

Mubarakpuri, Safiur Rahman (1995) "The Sealed Nectar" (Ar-Raheeq Al-Makhtum), Lahore: Al-Maktba Alsalfia.

Muhammad ibn Ishaq, (2004) The Life of Muhammad, Oxford University Press, Karachi.

Nadvi, Sulaiman Hussaini (2205) Khutbat-e-Seerat, Karachi: Zam-Zam Publishers.

Noamani, Shibli and Syed Solaiman Nadhvi (2004) Seeratun-Nabi, Karachi: Dharul-Ishaat.

Pea, Roy D. (2015) What Is Planning Development the Development of? Accessed: April 2015, http://web.stanford.edu/~roypea/RoyPDF%20folder/A11_Pea_82d.pdf

Peter H. Langford, Cameron B. Dougall, Louise P. Parkes, (2017) "Measuring leader behaviour: evidence for a "big five" model of leadership", Leadership & Organization Development Journal, Vol. 38 Issue: 1, pp.126-144, https://doi.org/10.1108/LODJ-05-2015-0103

Phalwari, Muhammad Jaafer (1995) Peghambr-e-Insaniat, Lahore: Idara Sakafat-e-Islamia.

Razi, Muhammad Wali (1987) Hadhi-e-Alam, Dharul-Ilm: Karachi.

Robbins, Stephen, and Mary Coulter (2017) Management, New Delhi: Pearson Education.

Saani, Javed Iqbal (2017) Prophet (ﷺ) Muhammad (ﷺ) as a planning expert, London: Intellectual Capital Enterprise Limited.

Saani, Javed Iqbal (2016) Responsibilities of Managers: Selected Ahadith, available on amazon.co.uk. (Paperback edition)

Schumpeter, J. A. (1934). *Theory of Economic Development*. Cambridge, MA: Harvard University Press.

Shoqi, Abu Khalil (2002) Atlas-Seerat-e-Nabvi, Darussalam: Lahore.

Siddiqi, Naeem (1997) The Benefactor of Humanity (Mohsin-e-Insaniyat), Dehli: Markazi Matabah Islami Publishers.

Smith, Mike (2007) Fundamentals of Management, Berkshire: McGraw Hill Education.

Stogdill, R.M. (1957), Leader Behaviour: Its Description and Measurement, Bureau of Business Research, College of Commerce and Administration, Ohio State University, Columbus.

Time Management Guide (2015) What is planning and why you need to plan, Accessed: April 2015, http://www.time-management-guide.com/planning.html

Books of Ahadith

Imam Muhammad ibn Isma`il al-Bukhari al-Ju`fi (1983) Sahih Al-Bukhari, Translated by Muhammad Muhsin Khan, Lahore: Kazi Publications.

Imam Muhammad ibn Isma`il al-Bukhari al-Ju`fi (1983) Al-Adab al-Mufrad, www.darsusalam.com

Imâm Abut Hussain Muslim bin al-Hajjaj, SahIh Muslim, Translated by Nasiruddin al-Khattab, Riyadh, 2007, Maktaba Dar-us-Salam.

Imam Muslim ibn al-Ḥajjāj al-Qushayrī (1971-75) Translated by Abdul Hameed Siddiqui Sahih Muslim, Lahore, Sh. Muhammad Ashraf.

lmâm Hâfiz Abu Dawud, Sunan Abu Dawud Sulaiman bin Ash'ath, Maktaba Dar-us-Salam, Riyadh, 2007.

Imäm Hãfiz Abü 'Elsa Mohammad Ibn 'Elsa At-Tirmidhi, Jamia' At-Tirmıdhi, English Translation by Abu Khaliyl, Riyadh, 2007, Maktaba Dar-us-Salam.

Imiim Hiifiz Abu Abdur Rahmiin Ahmad bin Shu'aib bin 'Ali An-Nasa'i, Sunan An-Nasa'i, Riyadh, 2007, Maktaba Dar-us-Salam.

Imam Muhammad Bin Yazeed Ibn Majah Al-Qazwinf, Sunan Ibn Majah Translated by Nasiruddin al-Khattab, Riyadh, 2007, Maktaba Dar-us-Salam.

Abu Zakaria Al-Nawawi, Riyad-us-Saliheen, Riyadh, 2007, Maktaba Dar-us-Salam.

Imam Malik bin Ans (رضي الله عنه), Muwatta Imam Malik, translated in Urdu by Allama Molana Abdul Hakeem Akhtar Shahjahanpuri, Lahore: Fareed Book Stall, accessed on 14 November 2017, https://readingpk.com/muwatta-imam-malik-imam-muhammad-malik/
https://www.sunnah.com

INDEX

A

Abbaas, *38, 40, 41*
Abd Allah Ibn Rawahah, 29
Abdurrehman Bin Ouff (RA), 66
Abu Bakr (RA), 66
Abu Hadhadh Aslami (RA), 57
Abu Sufyan, *38, 40, 42, 45, 46*
Abu'd-Darda, Ix
Al-Bukhari, 100
Al-E-Imran, Xi
Ali (RA), 30, 65
Allah (SWT), Ix, Xi, Xiii, Xiv, Xv, Xix, Xxi, 29, 42, 53, 54, 57, 60, 61, 63, 66, 70, 71, 72, 75, 76, 77, 84, 90, 116
Amnesty, *42*
Anas, Ix
Animal, 69
Ansar, 53, 55, 60
Apostle, 53, 54
Appointed, Vii
Aqabah, 30
Arab, 64, 65, 67, 68
Asim Bin Addi (RA), 66

Association of Project Management, 68
At-Tirmidhi, ix
Australia, Vii
Az-Zumar, Ix
9, Ix

B

Baitul-Rizwan, 59
Banu Baker, *37, 44, 45*
Banu Khaza, *37, 44*
Battle, 37, 64, 67, 73
Battlefield, 53, 58
Book, Ii, Viii, 72, 117
Books, 114
Booty, 55, 56, 59, 60, 61
Bukhari, 100
Byzantine, 64

C

Camel, 69, 71
Camels, 60
Campaign, 65, 66, 70
Case *Study*, 115
Cause Of Allah, Xiii
Charity, Xv

Chief Executive Officer, 78, 79

Companions, Xxi, 66, 71, 72, 73, 74, 76, 77, 79, 80

Consult, Xi

Consultation, 75

Contributors, 66

Controlling, 114

D

Deakin University, Vii

Death, Xiv

Decision, 56, 57

Decision Making, 56

Deputy, 74, 78

Dissemination, 58

Divine, 73, 77

E

Education, Xvii

Effectively, 68, 72

Efficiently, 72

Empire, 64

Enemy, 52, 53, 55, 56, 57, 58, 60

Expedition, 56, 66, 67, 68, 70, 71, 72

F

Fazail-E-Amaal, Xi, 98

Finance, Vii

Forgiveness, ix, Xi, Xxi, Xxii, 54

Formal Network, 68

G

Goats, 60

God, Xi, 30

Gratitude, Xix

H

Hajj, 117

Haris Bin Kaldhah (RA), 59

Hawazin, *39, 43, 46, 47*

Haykal, *44, 49, 98*

Helpers, 55, 59, 61

Hijrah, 98, 113

Hodhabia, 37, 38, 43, 45, 73, 75, 77, 79, 113

Hozan, 51

Hudaibiyah, 73, 77

Hudhaifah, 28

Hunain, 51, 52, 53, 56, 58, 113

Hypocrites, 65, 69, 70, 72

I

Informal Systems, 68

Information, Xix, *43, 44, 46, 48,* 56, 57, 58, 67, 68, 70, 71, 72, 77, 78

Information Management, 56

Innovation, 97

International Journals, Vii

104

Iqbal, Xxii

IQRA University Islamabad, Vii

Islam, 76, 77, 111

Islamic, Vii, 70, 111, 116, 119

Islamic Army, *39, 42*

Islamic Leadership Style, Vii

J

Javed Iqbal Saani, I, Ii, Xxii, 113, 114

Jeeranah, 55

Journey, 66, 71

K

Kaaba, 76

Ka'bah, 74

Kandhelvi, *38, 40*

Khalid, *39, 40, 42, 46*

Khalidh Bin Waleedh (RA), 67

Khandaq, I

Khaybar, 27

Khaza, 75, 76

Knowledge, Ix, X

L

Land, 69

Leader, Xi

Leaders, 60

Leadership, 99

Leading, 114

Learning, Vii

Lings, 31, *38, 39, 42, 46, 47*, 66, 70, 74, 98

London, I, Ii, 97, 99, 113, 114

M

Maaviya Bin Abu Sufyan (RA), 59

Madhina, *39, 44, 49*

Madinah, 55, 64, 65, 66, 67, 68, 74, 78, 79, 89

Makkah, *37, 38, 39, 41, 42, 43, 45, 46, 48, 49, 51, 52, 57*, 65, 66, 68, 74, 75, 76, 78, 79, 113

Management, Vii, 78, 97, 98, 99, 100, *111*, 112, 113, *114, 115*, 119, 135

Management Sciences, Vii

Manager, Xi

Managerial Implications, *43*

Managers, 67, 70

Managers, 25, 99, 114, 115

Manpower, 65

Marketing, 114

Masood Bin Umar Ghaffari (RA), 59

Mecca, 27, 31, 47, 51, 71, 74, 85

Medina, 27, 28, 30, *38, 48*, 65

Merciful, Xiv

Mercy, Xi, Xv

Messages, 46

Messenger, Ix, Xv, 52, 54, 56

Messenger Of Allah, Ix, Xiii, Xv

Migration, 61

Motivation, Xxi

Mubarikpuri, *42, 45, 46, 48,* 64, 69

Muhammad, ix, Xi, 34, 41, 44, 49, 97, 98, 99, 100, 101, 114

Muhammad Bin Musalmah (RA), 66

Muntakhib Ahadith, Xii

Muslim, 64, 65, 67, 71, 100

Muslims, *37, 39, 42, 43, 44, 48, 49,* 51, *52,* 53, *55,* 57, 58, 59, 60, 61, 64, 65, 66, 67, 69, 70, 73, 75, 76, 77, 78, 80

N

Nabi, Xi, 98, 99

Najd, 28

Negotiation, 79

Neubert (2009), 97

O

Objectives, 70

Observation, 58

Organisation, 78

Organisations, 56

Organising, 114

Organization, Vii, 97

P

Paradise, Xiii

Parents, Xvii

Participants, 66, 68, 70

Performance, Vii

Phalwarvi, 70, 99

Pilgrimage, 74

Plan, 100

Planning, 65, 99, 100, 114

Prayers, Xvii, Xxi

Project, Xix

Prophet (ﷺ), X, Xiii, 52, 55, 56, 57, 58, 59, 60, 61, 64, 65, 66, 67, 68, 69, 70, 71, 72, 98, 99, 113, 114, 115, 116

Q

Quality, 67

Qur'an, Xi

Quraysh, *37, 39, 40, 41, 42, 43, 45, 46, 47, 48, 49,* 60, 73, 74, 75, 76, 77, 78, 79

R

Rasulullaah, Xi, *38, 40, 41*

Rawalakot, Vii

Research, Vii, 100

Research Proposal, Vii

Resources, 56, 65, 66, 69

106

Reward, Xix
Riyadh Us Salihin, X
Romans, 64, 65, 67

S

Saad Bin Ubaidhah (RA), 66
Saani, 99, 113
Safwaan Bin Ummiya (RA), 59
Sakeef, 51, 57
Salam, Xv
Salat, Xv
Shibli, 70
Shoqi, 99
Siddiqi, Naeem, 100
Soldier, 52, 60
Soldiers, 53, 60
Spoils Of War, 61
Stakeholders, 68, 72
Statistics, 69
Strategic, 97
Strategy, 67, 72
Subordinates, Xi
Suggestions, Xxii

T

Tabuk, 67, 70, 71
Tacit Knowledge, 69, 72
Taif, 53, 55, 58, 59, 61

Talha (RA), 66
Trench, 113
Tribes, 64, 65, 66, 67
Troops, 51, 52

U

Uhadh, 113
Umayr Bin Wahab, 32
Umer (RA), 66
Umm Salamah (RA), 74
Ummah, Xxi, Xxii
Umrah, 55, 74, 76, 79, 80
Usman (RA), 45, 66, 72, 75, 76, 79

V

Values, 57

W

Weapons, 52
Worship, X
Written Communication, 69
Written Record, 68, 72

Y

Yazeed Bin Abu Sufyan (RA), 59

Z

Zulhalifah, 74

OTHER BOOKS BY THE AUTHOR (S)

Islamic Management Style

1. Prof Dr. Javed Iqbal Saani (2020) **Introduction to Islamic Theory of Management**, Intellectual Capital Enterprise Limited, London, available on Amazon (Paperback edition)
2. Prof Dr. Javed Iqbal Saani (2020) **Problem Solving Approach of the Prophet [PBUH]**, Intellectual Capital Enterprise Limited, London, available on Amazon (Paperback edition)
3. Prof Dr. Javed Iqbal Saani (2020) **Managerial Implications of Five Pillars of Islam**, Intellectual Capital Enterprise Limited, London, available on Amazon (Paperback edition)
4. Prof Dr. Javed Iqbal Saani (2020) **Prophet (ﷺ) Muhammad's [PBUH] Selection of Team Leaders**, Intellectual Capital Enterprise Limited, London, available on Amazon (Paperback edition)
5. Prof Dr. Javed Iqbal Saani (2020) **Key Managerial Decisions of the Prophet (ﷺ) [PBUH]**, Intellectual Capital Enterprise Limited, London, available on Amazon (Paperback edition)
6. Prof Dr. Javed Iqbal Saani (2020) **Prophet (ﷺ) Muhammad [PBUH] & Evolution of Management Theory**, Intellectual Capital Enterprise Limited, London, available on Amazon (Paperback edition)
7. Prof Dr. Javed Iqbal Saani (2020) **Transformation Strategy of the Prophet (ﷺ) [PBUH]**, Intellectual

Capital Enterprise Limited, London, available on Amazon (Paperback edition)

8. Prof Dr. Javed Iqbal Saani (2020) **Managerial Implications of the Conquest of Khyber**, Intellectual Capital Enterprise Limited, London, available on Amazon (Paperback edition)
9. Prof Dr. Javed Iqbal Saani (2019) **Financial Management Strategy of the Prophet (ﷺ) (PBUH)**, Intellectual Capital Enterprise Limited, London, available on Amazon (Paperback edition)
10. Prof Dr. Javed Iqbal Saani (2019) **Information Management Strategy of the Prophet (ﷺ) (PBUH)**, Intellectual Capital Enterprise Limited, London, available on Amazon (Paperback edition)
11. Prof Dr. Javed Iqbal Saani (2019) **Motivation Strategy of the Prophet (ﷺ) (PBUH)**, Intellectual Capital Enterprise Limited, London, available on Amazon (Paperback edition)
12. Prof Dr. Javed Iqbal Saani (2019) **Strategic Management: The Approach of the Prophet (ﷺ) (PBUH)**, Intellectual Capital Enterprise Limited, London, available on Amazon (Paperback edition)
13. Prof Dr. Javed Iqbal Saani (2019) **Managerial Implications of the Major Expeditions of the Prophet (ﷺ) [PBUH]**, Intellectual Capital Enterprise Limited, London, available on Amazon (Paperback edition)
14. Prof Dr. Javed Iqbal Saani (2019) **Managerial Implications of the Major Military Expeditions of the Prophet (ﷺ) [PBUH]**, Intellectual Capital Enterprise Limited, London, available on Amazon (Paperback edition)
15. Prof Dr. Javed Iqbal Saani (2019) **Managerial Implications of the Major Non-Military Expeditions of the Prophet (ﷺ) [PBUH]**, Intellectual Capital Enterprise Limited, London, available on Amazon (Paperback edition)

16. Prof Dr. Javed Iqbal Saani (2019) **Managerial Implications of the Battle of Hodhabia**, Intellectual Capital Enterprise Limited, London, available on Amazon (Paperback edition)
17. Prof Dr. Javed Iqbal Saani (2019) **Managerial Implications of the Battle of Trench**, Intellectual Capital Enterprise Limited, London, available on Amazon (Paperback edition)
18. Prof Dr. Javed Iqbal Saani (2019) **Managerial Implications of the Conquest of Makkah**, Intellectual Capital Enterprise Limited, London, available on Amazon (Paperback edition)
19. Prof Dr. Javed Iqbal Saani (2019) **Managerial Implications of the Battle of Hunain**, Intellectual Capital Enterprise Limited, London, available on Amazon (Paperback edition)
20. Prof Dr. Javed Iqbal Saani (2019) **Managerial Implications of the Battle of Uhadh Campaign**, Intellectual Capital Enterprise Limited, London, available on Amazon (Paperback edition)
21. Prof Dr. Javed Iqbal Saani (2019) **Managerial Implications of the Tabuk Campaign**, Intellectual Capital Enterprise Limited, London, available on Amazon (Paperback edition)
22. Prof Dr. Javed Iqbal Saani (2019) **Management Practices of the Prophet (ﷺ)**, Intellectual Capital Enterprise Limited, London, available on Amazon (Paperback edition)
23. Prof Dr. Javed Iqbal Saani (2018) **Managerial Implications of the Hijrah Expedition**, Intellectual Capital Enterprise Limited, London, available on Amazon (Paperback edition)
24. Prof Dr. Javed Iqbal Saani (2018) **Managerial Implications of the Battle of BADR**, Intellectual Capital Enterprise Limited, London, available on Amazon (Paperback edition)
25. Prof Dr. Javed Iqbal Saani (2018) **Managerial Thoughts of the Prophet (ﷺ)** Intellectual Capital Enterprise Limited, London, available on Amazon (Paperback edition)

26. Prof Dr. Javed Iqbal Saani (2018) **Controlling Strategy of the Prophet (ﷺ)**, Intellectual Capital Enterprise Limited, London, available on Amazon (Paperback edition)
27. Prof Dr. Javed Iqbal Saani (2018) **Leading Strategy of the Prophet (ﷺ)**, Intellectual Capital Enterprise Limited, London, available on Amazon (Paperback edition)
28. Prof Dr. Javed Iqbal Saani (2018) **Organising Strategy of the Prophet (ﷺ)**, Intellectual Capital Enterprise Limited, London, available on Amazon (Paperback edition)
29. Prof Dr. Javed Iqbal Saani (2018) **Planning Strategy of the Prophet (ﷺ)**, Intellectual Capital Enterprise Limited, London, available on Amazon (Paperback edition)
30. Prof Dr. Javed Iqbal Saani (2017) **Prophet Muhammad (ﷺ) as a planning expert**, available on Amazon (Paperback edition)
31. Prof Dr. Javed Iqbal Saani (2017) **Sales and Marketing: Selected Ahadith**, available on amazon.co.uk. (Paperback edition)
32. Prof Dr. Javed Iqbal Saani (2016) **Responsibilities of Managers: Selected Ahadith**, available on amazon.co.uk. (Paperback edition)

[Please see the images of these books on the following pages in addition to my doctoral thesis]

Management Sciences

1. Prof Dr. Javed Iqbal Saani (2019) **Management Information Systems**, Intellectual Capital Enterprise Limited, London, available on Amazon (Paperback edition)
2. Prof Dr. Javed Iqbal Saani (2018) **Managing Your Projects**, Intellectual Capital Enterprise Limited, London, available on amazon.co.uk. (Paperback edition)

3. Prof Dr. Javed Iqbal Saani (2017) **Business Case Studies**, Intellectual Capital Enterprise Limited, London, available on Amazon (Paperback edition)
4. Prof Dr. Prof Dr. Javed Iqbal Saani (2016) **Research Proposals: Contents & Exemplars**, available on amazon.co.uk. (Paperback edition)
5. Prof Dr. Javed Iqbal Saani (2012) **Understanding Information Systems**, Manchester: GRaASS.
6. Prof Dr Javed Iqbal Saani (2011) **Digital Divide in South Asia**, ISBN: 9789699578120.
7. Prof Dr. Javed Iqbal Saani and Muhammad Rafi Khattak (2011) **Managing Risk in Projects**, ISBN: 9789699578090.
8. Prof Dr. Javed Iqbal Saani and Muhammad Nadeem Khan (2011, 2018) **Understanding Project Management**, ISBN: 978969957845, available on Amazon (Paperback edition)
9. Prof Dr. Javed Iqbal Saani (2011) **Information Systems for Managers**, Grass Books, Manchester.
10. Prof Dr. Javed Iqbal Saani (2010) **Managing strategic change: a real-world case study**, ISBN: 978-3838330952, available on amazon.co.uk. (Paperback edition)

General interest

1. Prof Dr. Javed Iqbal Saani (2020) **Islamic Perspective of Knowledge**, Intellectual Capital Enterprise Limited, London, available on Amazon (Paperback edition)
2. Prof Dr. Javed Iqbal Saani (2019) **The Intercession of the Prophet (ﷺ) (PBUH)**, Intellectual Capital Enterprise Limited, London, available on Amazon (Paperback edition)

3. Prof Dr. Javed Iqbal Saani (2019) **Who are Wrongdoers [Zalimoon]?** Intellectual Capital Enterprise Limited, London, available on Amazon (Paperback edition)

4. Prof Dr. Javed Iqbal Saani (2019) **Characteristics of Successful People**, Intellectual Capital Enterprise Limited, London, available on Amazon (Paperback edition)

5. Prof Dr. Javed Iqbal Saani (2019) **Key Campaigns of the Prophet [PBUH]**, Intellectual Capital Enterprise Limited, London, available on Amazon (Paperback edition)

6. Prof Dr. Javed Iqbal Saani (2019) **The Importance of Islamic Greeting**, Intellectual Capital Enterprise Limited, London, available on Amazon (Paperback edition)

7. Prof Dr. Javed Iqbal Saani (2019) **Who are Mujrimoon: Criminals, Polytheists & Sinners?** Intellectual Capital Enterprise Limited, London, available on Amazon (Paperback edition)

8. Prof Dr. Javed Iqbal Saani (2019) **GLAD TIDINGS of Allah (SWT) and His Apostle (PBUH) TO NOBLE PEOPLE**, Intellectual Capital Enterprise Limited, London, available on Amazon (Paperback edition)

9. Prof Dr. Javed Iqbal Saani (2019) **Qualities of Righteous People**, Intellectual Capital Enterprise Limited, London, available on Amazon (Paperback edition)

10. Prof Dr. Javed Iqbal Saani (2019) **Greatness of Allah (SWT) in the Words of Allah (SWT)**, Intellectual Capital Enterprise Limited, London, available on Amazon (Paperback edition)

11. Prof Dr. Javed Iqbal Saani (2019) **Tablighi Mazaakry: The Programme & Contents of the Work of Dawah**, Intellectual Capital Enterprise Limited, London, available on Amazon (Paperback edition)
12. Prof Dr. Javed Iqbal Saani (2018) **Qualities of Momins: The Quranic Perspective**, Intellectual Capital Enterprise Limited, London, available on Amazon (Paperback edition)
13. Prof Dr. Javed Iqbal Saani (2018) **Hajj Experience: Combining Dawah and Manasiks**, Intellectual Capital Enterprise Limited, London, available on Amazon (Paperback edition)
14. Prof Dr. Javed Iqbal Saani (2018) **Sukhn-e-Saani (The book of poetry)**, Intellectual Capital Enterprise Limited, London, available on Amazon (Paperback edition)
15. Prof Dr. Javed Iqbal Saani (2017) **Virtues of Sickness: Selected Ahadith**, available on Amazon (Paperback edition)
16. Prof Dr. Javed Iqbal Saani (2017) **Muhammad (PBUH): His Trials & Tribulations**, available on Amazon (Paperback edition)
17. Prof Dr. Javed Iqbal Saani (2016) **Experience: The Journey of My Life**, available on amazon.co.uk. (Paperback edition)

Islamic Management Style

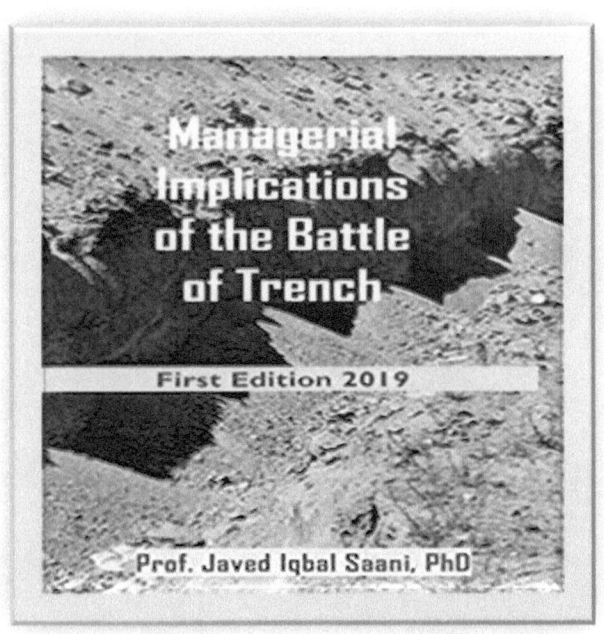

Management Sciences

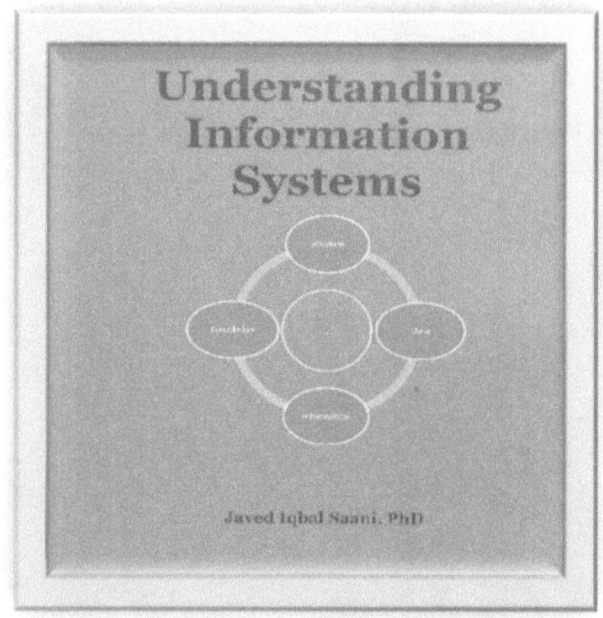

General Interest

ICE Series in General Interest

Islamic Perspective of Knowledge

PROF. JAVED IQBAL SAANI, PHD

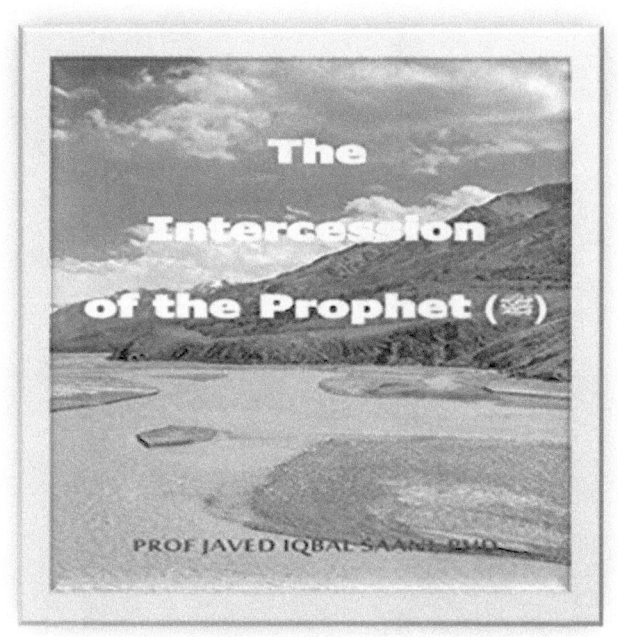

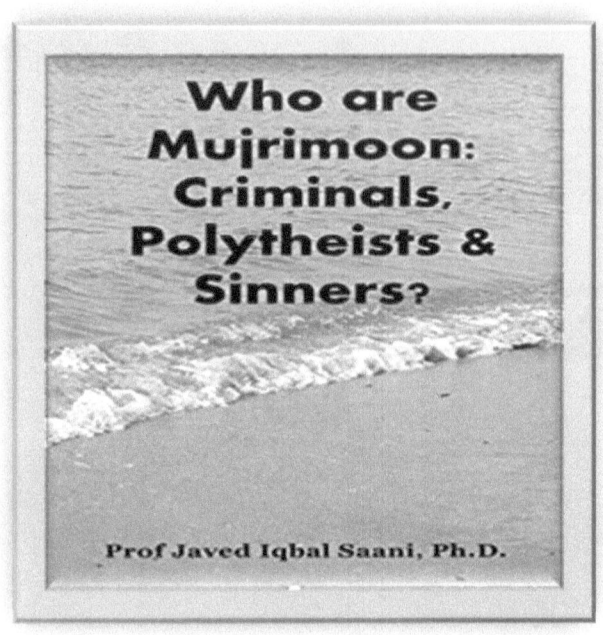

The Importance of ISLAMIC Greeting

اَلسَّلَامُ عَلَيْكُم

Prof Javed Iqbal Saani, Ph.D.

GLAD TIDINGS of Allah (SWT) and His Apostle (ﷺ) TO NOBLE PEOPLE

Prof Javed Iqbal Saani, Ph.D.

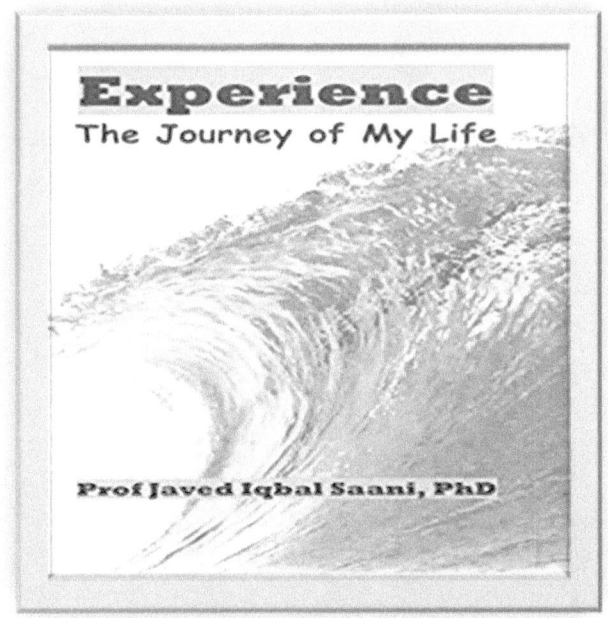

NOTES

www.ingramcontent.com/pod-product-compliance
Lightning Source LLC
Chambersburg PA
CBHW021417210526
45463CB00001B/415